D1595894

NURSES
—IN—
VIETNAM

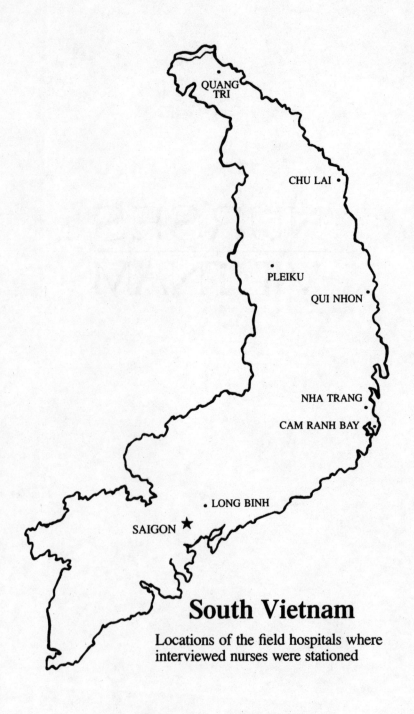

QUANG
TRI •

CHU LAI •

• PLEIKU

QUI NHON •

NHA TRANG •

CAM RANH BAY •

• LONG BINH

SAIGON ★

South Vietnam

Locations of the field hospitals where
interviewed nurses were stationed

NURSES
IN
VIETNAM
THE
FORGOTTEN
VETERANS

EDITOR: DAN FREEDMAN
ASSOCIATE EDITOR:
JACQUELINE RHOADS

★

TexasMonthlyPress

Texas Monthly Press, Inc.
P.O. Box 1569
Austin, Texas 78767

   B C D E F G H

Library of Congress Cataloging-in-Publication Data

Nurses in Vietnam.

   Includes index.
   1. Vietnamese Conflict, 1961–1975—Personal
narratives, American. 2. Vietnamese Conflict, 1961–1975
—Medical care. 3. Nurses—United States—Biography.
4. Nurses—Vietnam—Biography.   I. Freedman, Dan,
1952–   II. Rhoads, Jacqueline, 1948–
DS559.5.N87   1987   959.704′37   86-30104
ISBN 0-87719-047-X

Text design by David Timmons

This book is dedicated to the eight names on the wall:

1st Lt. Sharon Ann Lane
2nd Lt. Elizabeth Ann Jones
2nd Lt. Carol Ann Elizabeth Drazba
Lt. Col. Annie Ruth Graham
Capt. Eleanor Grace Alexander
1st Lt. Hedwig Diane Orlowski
2nd Lt. Pamela Dorothy Donovan
Capt. Mary Therese Klinker

They gave their lives so that others might live.

Contents

Acknowledgments

The seed of *Nurses in Vietnam* germinated during a walk I took one muddy afternoon at North Fort Hood, Texas, in June of 1984. Jacqueline Rhoads, an Army reservist and nursing school professor I had met while researching a magazine article on female Vietnam veterans, was dredging up remembrances of incidents that had occurred close to 15 years before. Many of these memories hadn't entered her mind since her return from Vietnam. All it took was: "You know, you ought to do a book about this." So we started from there and expanded. The oral histories contained in this volume come from nine nurses speaking only for themselves. They are not meant to be representative of all nurses who were in Vietnam. Rather, this book is a modest contribution to the growing body of literature on this both tragic and fascinating chapter of American history. While this is a book about Army nurses, it should be noted that Air Force and Navy nurses also served in Vietnam with distinction.

During the time most of these nine women were in Vietnam, I was a high school student in New York City. Along with thousands of others, I was actively opposed to the war. I spent a good chunk of my adolescence marching in demonstrations, distributing leaflets, and organizing boycotts, moratoriums and the wearing of black armbands—anything that I thought would hasten the end of the war and promote the vague radical agenda that captivated so many of us at the time. Now, years later, listening to these women and learning how they perceived that era's turmoil has personally helped me understand the time during which I grew to maturity—U.S. bombs started dropping on North Vietnam when I was in high school; the last American troops were pulled out when I was a junior in college. Knowing what I know now, I'm not sure I'd have done anything differently. Certainly any protester who spat on a returning veteran deserves condemnation. Yet I'd like to think that for every such case, there were others that demonstrated concern for the average man (and woman) on the battlefield who suffered because of the shortsightedness of politicians and generals.

Whatever the case, I do not want this book to be viewed either as an anti-war statement or an apology for the war. The fact that it contains elements that could be interpreted either way speaks to the ambiguity over Vietnam that is still with us.

In addition to Jacque and the eight other participants, there are a number of other personal acknowledgments I'd like to make. First is to my family, my wife, Mary Anne Hess, and my children, Sasha Johnson, Jacob Freedman and Andrew Freedman. They lived through this book word by word, and I can only hope that its final publication offsets the toll it took on our family. Also, in a general way, I owe an incalculable debt to my parents, Alfred and Marcia Freedman, and my brother, Paul Freedman, for their lifelong belief in my abilities.

Rose Sandecki, an outspoken veterans counselor in Concord, California, has given me long-distance encouragement and support since I became interested in the subject of women in Vietnam three years ago. Mary Stout of Vietnam Veterans of America was ready to help tie up loose ends as the book neared publication. Rick Sonntag of the Army Health Services Command dug up crucial data on nurse training at Fort Sam Houston. Anyone who has concerned themselves with the role of women in Vietnam cannot forget that it was Lynda Van Devanter who was the first to bring the subject to public attention with her book *Home Before Morning*. She is a true trailblazer.

The book would not have lifted off had it not been for the newspaper where I work, the *San Antonio Light*. Ted Warmbold, Ed Rademaekers and Jeff Cohen deserve special thanks for making the *Light* the kind of newspaper that could nurture a project such as this. Fred Blevens, a former *Light* editor who handed me a wire story about women in Vietnam and asked me to "localize" it (thus perking my interest in the subject), also deserves credit. John Wilburn, the former editor of *Viva,* the *Light's* Sunday magazine, had the vision necessary to guide this story into print the first time. The *Viva* piece was an important step along the way to this book's publication.

Also at the *Light,* there were a number of people who either gave me verbal shoulders to lean on, or who—because of the lack of privacy common to most newsrooms—were obligated to take messages and listen in on phone conversations concerning the book. In no particular order, the incomplete list would include: Gail Rosenblum, Melissa Fletcher, Ron Goins, Keri Guten, Sarah Pattee, Betty Godfrey, Mary Ann Horne, Sallyanne Holtz, Reneta Byrne, Enedelia Obregon, Kathy O'Connell, John Darkow, Joe Carroll Rust, David Hawkings, Cary Cardwell, Don Yaeger, Kevin Johnson, Marty Thompson, John Cochran.

Perhaps the largest debt is to Peggy Campbell, the woman who transcribed hours of what must have seemed like trivial and boring interviews onto computer diskettes. Without her patience and fortitude, I could not have pulled together this book and kept my job.

At Texas Monthly Press, Scott Lubeck and Anne Norman never lost their sense of humor nor their therapeutic touch when dealing with me. Their visions of this book never failed to match (and sometimes exceed) those of Jacque and myself.

Dan Freedman
San Antonio, Texas
September 1986

The nurses whose histories are reflected in this book had the courage and dedication to share their experiences in Vietnam with strangers. The telling of their stories surely opened up old wounds and made them relive that part of their life which is so sacred. I thank them and hope Dan and I have justified their trust.

In addition to these nurses I'd like to thank Dan Freedman, for he took my dream and made it a reality. He was gracious, kind, and so very open to the nurses' experiences. I feel because of his openness he has learned more about the true essence of nursing than anyone I know.

My family support must be acknowledged. My Mom and Dad (Florine and Joseph Navarra), brother and sister (Joe and Yvonne), stood behind me when I made the decision to go to Vietnam. Even though they were afraid for me, their support and faith were never ending. I still feel this love and support.

The six Passarell brothers, Edward, Dean, Roosevelt, Anthony, William, Adolph (my uncles), served in World War II and constantly encouraged, enlightened, and inspired me. How many nieces can say she had six uncles, all from the same family, who volunteered their services to their country during a World War? One of these uncles in particular needs mentioning.

He was wounded on the battlefield in the South Pacific and his experiences as he was triaged from the front lines back home were heart-rendering. All through my life, as well as my brother's and sister's lives, this wonderful man has been a role model, mentor, counselor, and best friend. At times when I knew I couldn't share some feelings with other members of my family I knew I could talk to him—that he'd understand, and he always has. His name is Roosevelt (Obell) Passarell.

My husband James was, and is, truly an inspiration to me. He listened, he responded, he supported me through this endeavor and never failed to encourage me when times were difficult; I could never begin to express how much I love him.

Last but not least, I'd like to mention my aunt Edna. When I first dreamed of becoming a nurse, my past school achievements made people believe I wouldn't be able to keep up the demands of nursing school. Even my parents worried about my future. My aunt Edna never doubted my capabilities. She stood behind me and helped me through very difficult times, never giving me a chance to fail. Even after graduation from nursing school, my aunt encouraged association with the US Army Nurse Corps and would write regularly wanting to know all I did. She was proud of my accomplishments. When I was in Vietnam, lonely and afraid, I would write to her of my fears and disappointments. She'd write back a "care message," making sure I understood that life isn't always easy and that these experiences would help me grow. After Vietnam, she never failed to "be there" when I had trouble adjusting—always pushing, encouraging, enlightening and loving me. In May of 1978 she died, but her presence is still with me and will be with me till I join her.

Jacqueline Rhoads
Albuquerque, New Mexico
September 1986

Introduction

A mong the more than 58,000 names carved on the wall of the Vietnam Veterans Memorial in Washington, D.C., are those of eight women. Their names are interspersed among their male compatriots', a mute testimony to the sacrifices, suffering, and exhilaration that women shared during the eight years of major American troop commitment in Vietnam. Despite an upsurge in public interest in Vietnam and the veterans who fought there, relatively little attention has been given to the fact that 8,000 to 10,000 women served as well. They worked in all branches of the military as intelligence analysts, air traffic controllers, and supply clerks. But the vast majority were nurses—and the majority of those were part of the Army field hospital system, set up to funnel wounded American men from a nonexistent front line into a network of tent and Quonset hut installations, depending on the location in Vietnam where the men were wounded and the gravity of their conditions.

The collective experience of the Army Nurse Corps in Vietnam is a crucial component of the history of that war. In a technical sense, nurses carried out the ancillary duties the United States traditionally assigns to women in wartime. If they carried weapons, it was for self-defense only. If their hospital compounds came under attack, it was viewed as a fluke—hardly the central focus of enemy military strategy. But in a real sense, nurses were thoroughly integrated into all the contradictions of life in a combat zone in Vietnam. When giant double-rotor Chinook helicopters unloaded 100 or more litters at a time, women nurses often made the difference between life and

death. They were in the thick of it—inserting and suctioning endo-
tracheal tubes so men would not choke to death on their own blood,
separating burned clothing from burned skin when often it was impossible to tell the difference, having men's feet come off in their
hands as they removed the men's boots.

Nurses transcended the prescibed role of passive observer. The
staggering tasks they confronted were not confined to treating combat wounds of Americans. In addition, there were the psychiatric
and drug cases, the men with parasitic diseases and malaria,
wounded Vietnamese civilians (frequently victims of American air
strikes), and hostile Vietnamese prisoners and civilians. Nurses
were not on patrol in the jungle, but when men were ambushed or
stepped on land mines, women often became front-line therapists—
the first ones to help GIs cope with the magnitude of the trauma that
had befallen them. Nurses fought the war—in their own fashion.

The emotional baggage that male veterans brought home has received a good deal of attention. Of the 2.8 million who served in
Vietnam, an estimated 500,000 to 800,000 suffer some form of
emotional problem. Surprisingly, there were relatively fewer psychiatric casualties during the Vietnam War than in other recent wars
involving massive numbers of American troops. The rate in Vietnam (12 per 1,000 troops) compares favorably with World War II
(101 per 1,000) and the Korean War (37 per 1,000). What is different
is that in Korea and World War II the incidence of psychiatric problems corresponded to the intensity of the war. As the war wound
down, the rate of psychiatric cases among soldiers also declined. By
contrast, mental disorders increased in the early 1970s as Americans
began withdrawing from Vietnam. The rate continued to spiral up-
ward as the soldiers turned into veterans.

The problems of male veterans are clouded by media-projected
images ranging from "Rambo," the can-do American avenging an-
gel in Vietnam, to news accounts of the occasional veteran-turned-
psychopath, playing out the jungle war back home with the lives of
innocent Americans. The nation, which to a large extent turned its
back on the men it had sent into combat, is now equally guilty of
manipulating the reality of their sacrifices. Whatever the gravity of
the problem, the issue is slowly being addressed. In the late 1970s,
the Veterans Administration set up a chain of Vet Centers nation-

wide to offer psychological and career counseling to veterans. The Vietnam memorial, the addition of a Vietnam Unknown Soldier at Arlington National Cemetery, and the numerous parades of fatigue-clad men have all served to instill a fresher, more positive image of Vietnam veterans in the minds of most Americans.

In comparison, relatively less hoopla has accompanied the recognition of women Vietnam veterans. A few books, a television documentary, and scattered newspaper feature stories are the only public manifestations that, yes, women also were in Vietnam and, yes, they too suffered many of the same problems affecting male veterans. The federal government has been slow to recognize that women exhibit many of the same side effects of service in Vietnam, though perhaps the causes are different.

Post-traumatic stress disorder (known as PTSD in veteran and psychological counseling circles) only made its way back into the psychiatric *Diagnostic and Statistical Manual of Mental Disorders* in 1980, after a 12-year absence. PTSD is roughly defined as a special form of anxiety disorder marked by an identifiable "stressor" (such as war service), flashbacks, problems sleeping, and a sense of guilt about surviving when others did not. Veterans Administration counselors initially did not consider women Vietnam veterans capable of suffering this disorder because, they reasoned, women were not in combat.

It took a long time for those at the top to realize that being a combination emergency technician, confessor and mother figure to masses of wounded men caused the same kind of stress as being in combat. An indication of the extent of suffering by women Vietnam veterans came in the wake of Jenny Ann Schnaier's pioneering study, completed as a master's thesis in 1982, in which a survey of 87 women veterans uncovered extensive stress symptoms. "The results indicated that approximately one-third of the [different] stress symptoms [associated with PTSD] were endorsed by 25 percent of the subjects, and of symptoms first reported as having occurred between homecoming and one year after Vietnam, approximately 70 percent were reported as still present," Schnaier wrote.

It would be wrong, however, to conclude that women veterans suffer the same as men. In fact, the kind of women who went to Vietnam were extremely different from the men who went; so it stands to reason that, despite some common symptoms, their post-war experiences will be different too. Generally, women serving in Vietnam were better educated and older than the men. Nurses had completed nursing school, so the youngest women were likely to be over 21. The average age of men serving in Vietnam, according to a number of studies, was 19.

Nurses were volunteers. They went to Vietnam for a variety of reasons: professional commitment, patriotism, and above all else a desire to serve in a situation that most would probably remember as the ultimate challenge of their nursing careers. It was a situation that promised to be rife with contradictions. Many had doubts about the American presence in Vietnam. Handling the war's human toll day in and day out only accentuated a deep-rooted sense of pointlessness and waste. On the other hand, as nurses they were doing things they could never hope to do in the rigidly structured civilian hospital world, where deference to doctors and strict delineation of doctors' and nurses' duties constituted a seemingly permanent work agenda.

In Vietnam, nurses were closing wounds after surgery, doing emergency tracheotomies by themselves, starting IVs, and administering medications with hardly a glance from male doctors. Back home, many would remember or soon find out that giving an aspirin was considered beyond the nurse's domain. So Vietnam represented the summit of professionalism, the peak from which every other nursing experience would seem to pale in comparison. The contrast inspired many to go back to school and earn bachelor's, master's, and even doctoral degrees in nursing. Such degrees enabled them to rise above much of the drudgery that accompanies basic nursing in a civilian setting. But others left nursing altogether.

Hand in hand with a sense of achievement went the frustration of working in an Army field hospital. Zealous in their convictions that the Army could provide the ultimate challenge to their care-giving skills, nurses soon discovered that Vietnam did not resemble the cinematic version of World War II with which they had grown up. This was not a war where a soldier could be wounded heroically, hurling a grenade at an enemy pillbox before being cut down by withering machine gun fire. Rather, Vietnam was a place where thousands lost limbs from land mines, where there was neither front nor rear, and where a combatant rarely saw the enemy he was attempting to shoot.

This different kind of war brought into existence an entirely new way of treating the wounded. High-powered rifle blasts did not produce neat little holes. The shells ricocheted through flesh, ripping organs and tissue along the way. Medevac helicopters were in Korea, but their use was perfected in Vietnam. The Huey dust-off flights may have inadvertently compounded the difficulty of treating wounded in a field hospital. The helicopter could swoop down and deliver casualties to the hospital within minutes. As a result, many who would have died in previous wars were kept alive with gauze pads, intravenous connections, and tracheal tubes. Many, however, would not make it. They arrived alive in a technical sense, but dead to the world. Some required neurosurgery too extensive to undertake while other more salvageable cases were pouring through the hospital. Better to save four whose wounds were mendable than one who might tie up the operating room for hours and die anyway, the logic went. This, then, was the basis for triage, or "playing God" as some nurses came to call it.

For women whose careers were built around saving lives, the inability to forestall death was sometimes hard to take. Serious head and chest wounds were put into the "expectant" category, a military euphemism for those left to die. The nurse's mission to save and heal often was no match for mounds of gored and dismembered human flesh and bones. Even so, the experience of nurses in Vietnam amounted to a coexistence of positive and negative elements. The women who participated in the Schnaier study, while reporting a recurrence of stress symptoms, also accented positive experiences they felt helped to propel their careers along. All memory is selective and it is conceivable that veterans justify the good or bad aspects of their wartime experience depending on their current circumstances.

Coping with stress is not the only issue confronting women veterans today. Until female veterans, in groups and individually, mounted a reform campaign, Veterans Administration facilities for women were woefully inadequate. A General Accounting Office study, issued in 1982, found that the VA was, in essence, discriminating against female veterans because hospital wards, treatment programs, and outpatient services were geared exclusively toward male veterans. The GAO discovered that women with non-service related medical concerns were given short shrift at VA hospitals while men with the same medical problems were treated as a matter of routine.

Congressional hearings called to consider legislation creating an advisory committee to the Veterans Administration on women veterans' affairs uncovered more VA horror stories. One woman recalled passing out in a car in Brooklyn, N.Y., and going to the veterans hospital at Fort Hamilton. There the doctors diagnosed her as pregnant, even though she was single and insisted that she had not engaged in sexual activity. Nevertheless, the hospital was unable to do the tests necessary to confirm pregnancy because it had no program for gynecological care. Bureaucratic delays in securing an appointment with a gynecologist at another VA hospital led to an emergency operation—a partial hysterectomy. Doctors found an umbilical hernia and enlarged fibroid tumors. The woman was not pregnant.

The VA has gone to considerable lengths to acknowledge the special needs of women veterans. Since the hearings, the VA has rebuilt several of its older facilities to accommodate the privacy requirements of women patients. Over the next four years, the VA has earmarked $6.2 million for similar construction projects at 40 of its 172 hospitals.

Women are also active in the fight to get the government to recognize that they too have suffered from exposure to the chemical herbicide Agent Orange. Post-war disabilities ranging from breast tumors to miscarriages have been attributed to Agent Orange. Several former Red Cross volunteers (all civilians) are spearheading a drive to get the federal Center for Disease Control to study the effects of Agent Orange on women. The CDC is already studying links between Agent Orange and male veterans, as is the Air Force. Females who were in the military are entitled to apply for a share in the $180 million out-of-court settlement reached in 1984 between veterans and Agent Orange manufacturers. Red Cross civilians, however, have no such recourse.

Also, a group of women veterans based in Minnesota is undertaking a campaign to raise $1 million for a bronze statue of a nurse to stand alongside the one of three men at the Washington, D.C., Vietnam memorial. The model created by sculptor Roger Brodin depicts a woman in fatigues and boots, with a hemostat and cast scissors in her pocket, carrying her helmet. The statue looks tired—tired of the long hours, the heat, the war in general. The Minnesota group is confident that it will secure federal approval of the project. The target dedication date is Veterans Day of 1987.

The nursing profession has its roots in wartime service. The western world's two most famous nurses, Florence Nightingale and Clara Barton, won recognition for their pioneering efforts to organize and treat the wartime wounded in an efficient and sanitary way. During the Revolutionary War, by contrast, wounded men depended on the untrained civilian population for care. Wives, sisters, and mothers often followed their soldier relatives into battle and cared for them if they fell.

The Civil War saw the establishment of professionalized (though primitive) medical treatment of wounded soldiers. Clara Barton, who later founded the Red Cross, ministered to Union soldiers in Washington, D.C., during the Civil War. Dorthea L. Dix, who also won a name crusading for reform in psychiatric institutions, served as Superintendent of Women Nurses, leading a team of approximately 6,000 women (including many Catholic nuns) who worked in Union hospitals.

The Civil War experience convinced American military officers that women were indispensable to any wartime effort. Nurses served under contract in the Spanish-American War. And by act of Congress in 1901, the Army Nurse Corps was established under the Army Medical Department. The Navy established its nurse corps in 1908. The Army and Navy combined had 23,000 nurses during World War I. Approximately 10,000 served overseas. They tended wounded Americans on ships and trains, and served in front-line aid stations and field hospitals.

It was in World War II that the military perfected the hospital evacuation system. Between the wars there had been significant advances in nursing education and medical treatment of wounds. The peak strength of the Army and Navy nurse corps combined was nearly 69,000. Even without substantial help from helicopters, Army medical teams developed a reasonably fast and efficient method for sustaining the wounded close to a mobile front line and ferrying them through a chain of hospitals behind the line to a place where they could receive the level of care appropriate to their individual conditions. Less seriously wounded soldiers could then return to the front line upon recovery, while more serious cases were shipped back home.

In World War II, nurses discovered their medical ranks did not necessarily guarantee them non-combatant status. Approximately 200 Army nurses died in combat. A total of 82 Army and Navy nurses were prisoners of war. In the Philippines in 1942, 11 Army nurses were taken prisoner when Manila fell to the Japanese. They spent 37 months in POW camps.

The Korean War saw the advent of medevac helicopters and aeromedical evacuation. These two elements were direct forerunners of the medical treatment system in Vietnam. In Korea, as in Vietnam, soldiers could be whisked off the battlefield by helicopter to an evacuation hospital. If their wounds were grave enough, they might have soon found themselves on a propeller-driven Air Force evacuation plane bound for home. Thanks to M*A*S*H in both its movie and television incarnations, the public at large was given a lampoontype exposure to the haphazard existence of nurses, doctors, and technicians in Army tent hospitals.

During the early- to mid-1960s, the Army Medical Department still had relatively recent experience in actual wartime casualty care. The Medical Field Service School at Fort Sam Houston in San Antonio, Texas, was the installation at which nurses and medical technicians received their military basic training after joining the Army. During the Vietnam War, approximately 9,410 nurses completed the six-week basic course there. Officials at Army Health Services Command at Fort Sam Houston estimate that 80 percent of those graduates were women. Nurse recruiting during Vietnam started slowly, with only 650 nurse recruits coming into the Army in 1965. By 1970 the figure peaked at 1,436, then declined to 395 in 1973.

After the war, a surprising number of nurses filtered back to San Antonio. The reasons varied. Some enjoyed the relaxed environment of the city they had discovered during basic training. Others followed Army friends who had already settled there. But the one thing they all found attractive was that, in San Antonio, they could live among their own kind. Approximately 55,000 Vietnam veterans live in the San Antonio area. According to 1980 census data, 5,160 women who were in the military during the Vietnam era lived in Bexar County, which includes San Antonio.

The census figure does not distinguish between women who actually served in Vietnam and women who were in the military in assignments other than Vietnam. Still, it is a good indication that the city holds a special appeal to female veterans. The state of Texas is home to the second highest number of female Vietnam veterans— 19,600 (compared to the leader, California with 32,800). San Antonio, with 5,160 female Vietnam-era veterans, claims more than a quarter of the state's total.

Besides the Alamo, the springtime Fiesta celebration, and the restaurant-lined Riverwalk, the city is known for its four Air Force bases and one Army post. The Chamber of Commerce proudly bills San Antonio as "Military City U.S.A.," while more waggish San Antonians traditionally have called it the "mother-in-law of the Army," a reference to the preponderance of local females who marry uniformed officers and enlisted men stationed there.

Because of its large active duty and retired military populations, San Antonio offered a relatively hospitable and understanding environment to veterans. This was important to veterans coming home to a nation indifferent to their sacrifices and insensitive to their need to talk. In San Antonio, they would not encounter the cold stares, the shrugs, or people saying "Oh, you were in Vietnam—that's nice," before moving on to another subject. Upon returning home, most veterans found what they needed above all else was people who would listen. They found those listeners among other veterans. In turn, they too became good listeners.

Most of the nine women who participated in this oral history live in and around San Antonio. None are native Texans. In one sense, they represent nobody but themselves. They demonstrate that each experience in Vietnam had its individual character. They did not all serve in exactly the same type of hospital setting. They did not all plummet to the same depths nor rise to the same heights.

But, in another sense, they are representative of the largely unexplored women's perspective on a war that defies general consensus to this day. The details of their experiences—and how those experiences affected their later lives—are all part of the mosaic of nurses in Vietnam. There is no pretense that recounting their experiences is anything more than an effort to add some tiles to that mosaic, to fill in some historical blanks, and hopefully to add a little information to the nation's understanding of what Vietnam meant—and continues to mean—to all of us.

Jacqueline Navarra Rhoads

We arrived in Vietnam on April 26, 1970, right in the middle of a rocket attack. We were ordered off the plane and everyone was supposed to lay down on the ground. So here I am with my dress uniform, stockings, shoes, and skirt, and suddenly I'm lying down on a cement pavement at Tan Son Nhut wondering, "My God, what did I get myself into?" The noise was so deafening. The heat—I remember how hot it was. We eventually got inside this terminal building where there were all these guys waiting to get on the plane to go home. They were whooping it up, running around with signs saying things like: "Only one hour and 35 minutes left!" They saw us coming and one of them said, "Cheer up, the worst is yet to come." We stayed there 16 hours before we could get out. When we got on the bus, all the windows were screened. I learned from the bus driver that this was to prevent the Vietnamese from throwing grenades in through the windows. I said, "But I thought the enemy was up north somewhere." He told me, "No, the enemy is all around you here. You never know who you're fighting."

My first assignment was in Phu Bai. I was there for 30 days because they needed some emergency room nurses there. Then I was

---

In Vietnam between 1970 and 1971, Jacqueline Navarra Rhoads spent most of her tour with the 18th Surgical Hospital in Quang Tri. Born in 1948, she grew up in Albion, New York. Formerly of San Antonio, she now resides in Albuquerque, New Mexico, where she is on the nursing faculty at the University of New Mexico.

transferred to the 18th Surgical Hospital at Quang Tri, just a few miles from the DMZ. They had just put a MUST (Medical Unit Self-Transportable) unit in there from Camp Evans and they needed operating and emergency room nurses right away. I was there the remainder of my tour.

I was a very young 21. At St. Mary's School of Nursing in Rochester (New York), I kept these Army recruiting posters all over my room. There was a big push at that time for nurses, and we had recruiters coming to the school constantly from the time I started in 1966. I don't know what it was, I loved nursing so much. I always thought—I know it sounds crazy—but I wanted to do something for my country. I just had a feeling that being a nurse in the Army was what I wanted to do. And of course my uncles were all in the Army in World War II. There were nine brothers in my mother's family, and they all went into the Army within six months of each other.

Everyone thought I was crazy. I remember my mother saying, "Jacque, do you know what you're getting yourself into?" Of course, when you're young you have no fear.

I did basic training at Fort Sam Houston in San Antonio. My main memory of that time is the parties, big parties. I never took basic training very seriously. It was only later I realized that I should have. What to do in case of a nuclear attack, what to do for chemical warfare, how to handle a weapon—these were things we laughed at. We went out to Camp Bullis and shot weapons, but as nurses we never thought that shooting a weapon was something we needed to know. True, we never had to fire weapons, but we had wounded who came in with weapons as splints, and they were loaded weapons. When that happened, I thought, "Why didn't I listen when they taught us how to take this weapon apart?" You know, an M-16 with a full magazine. We had a young guy come in, he had a grenade with the pin pulled wrapped in a handkerchief and stuffed into his fatigue pocket, a live grenade! I thought, "Gosh, if only I had listened."

I think the practice village out where we trained at Camp Bullis is still in existence. The bamboo sticks smeared with excrement, they were authentic. There was an instructor in black pajamas, camouflage makeup on his face. Well, we kind of laughed. We didn't take it seriously until we started seeing these kinds of injuries in Vietnam.

My first real exposure to the war came five days after I landed. It was at Phu Bai. We received 25 body bags in on this giant Chinook helicopter. You know, the Chinook is this great big helicopter, this two-blade deal that can carry 100–150 people. And this Chinook came in with 25 body bags aboard. One of the nurses' responsibilities was to look inside these body bags to determine cause of death. Of course, they couldn't release the doctors for such trivial work. What you had to do was open the bag, look inside and see what possibly could have killed this person, and then write down on the tag what you felt the cause of death was. It was so obvious most of the time. That's something I still have flashbacks about— unzipping those bags. It was my first exposure to maggots, something I had never seen before in my life.

One was a young guy who had had his face blown away, with hundreds of maggots eating away where his face used to be. Another one, he had his eyes wide open. He was staring up at me. I remember he had a large hole in his chest and I knew it was a gunshot wound or a grenade injury. It had blown his heart, his lungs, everything to shreds. He had nothing left but a rib cage. Evidently, they had lain out on the ground awhile before someone could get to them. The corpsmen were told to take care of the wounded first, instead of spending time getting the dead in the bags. There were GIs exposed to flame throwers or gas explosions. We used to call them "crispy critters" to keep from getting depressed. They'd come in and there would be nothing more than this shell of a person. That was a little easier to take, they didn't have a face. It could have been an animal's carcass for all you knew. But to have to go looking for the dog tags, to find the dog tags on a person, that bothered me. I remember the first time I looked in a body bag I shook so badly. One of the doctors was kind enough to help me through it, saying, "Come on, it's your duty and you're going to have to do this. It's just something that I'm going to help you through. It's just a dead person." It was such a close-knit group. We were considered the most beautiful women in the world. The guys treated us special. You could have been the ugliest woman in the world, but still you were treated special.

The mass-cal, that's mass-casualty situation, traditionally was anything more than 10 or 15 wounded. It was mass chaos, bordering on panic. There'd be a corpsman walking around saying, "Dust off just called and they're bringing in 25 wounded. Everybody get going." So we'd pull out all our supplies. The nurses would put extra tourniquets around their necks to get ready to clamp off blood vessels. The stretchers were all prepared, and we'd go down each row hanging IVs all plugged and ready to go. It was mass production. You'd start the IVs on those people where the doctor was able to say, "This one is saved, this one is saved." We put them in triage categories. The expectant ones were the ones who required too much care. We'd make them comfortable and allow them to die. I guess it was making us comfortable too.

I remember this guy named Cliff, a triple amputee we once had. He came in with mast-trousers on. Mast-trousers is an apparatus you inflate that puts pressure on the lower half of your body to allow adequate blood flow to your heart and brain. When Cliff came in, he was conscious, which was amazing. He looked like a stage dummy who'd been thrown haphazardly in a pile. One of his legs was up underneath his chin so that he was able to look down at the underside of his foot. His left arm was twisted behind his head in a horrible way. We couldn't even locate his second leg. He had stepped on a land mine. With his legs that bad, we knew there probably wasn't much backbone left. He was alive because of these trousers. The corpsman must have been right there when he got wounded. He had put him in this bag and inflated it. Cliff should have been dead.

It was really funny because he looked at two of us nurses there and said, "God, I think I've died and gone to heaven . . . a round-eye, an American, you look so beautiful." He was so concerned about the way he looked because of us standing there, "Gee, I must look a mess." But he was alert, he knew where he was. "Doc, take good care of me. I know my leg is pretty bad because I can see it, but take good care of me, doc." The docs couldn't put him in the expectant category and give him morphine to make him comfortable, because he was too alert. The docs had trouble letting go. So one of them finally said, "Well, let's get him into the operating room, deflate the bag, and let's get in there and see if we can't do something."

Well, we knew just by looking at him in that condition that he wasn't going to last, that as soon as we deflated the bag he'd bleed to death in a matter of seconds. Somehow, he knew it too. I remember I was getting blood prepared for him. He called me from across the room, "Jacque, come here quick." I went over to him and said, "What's the matter Cliff, what's wrong?" He said, "Just hold my hand and don't leave me." I said, "Why, Cliff? Are you in pain?" We always worried about pain, alleviating pain. We'd do anything to alleviate pain. He said, "I think I'm going to die and I don't want to be alone." So I stood there crying, with him holding my hand. And when we deflated the trousers, we lost him in seconds. We found no backbone, no lower part of his body. Really, he had been cut in half.

The leg that was folded underneath his neck was completely severed from his body. It was just there. The corpsmen had evidently bundled him together into the bag hoping maybe something would be there that was salvageable. And he just died. I remember he had blond hair, blue eyes—cute as a button. I had to take his body myself to graves registration. I just couldn't let him go alone. I just couldn't do that. I had to pry my hand away from his hand, because he had held on to my hand so tightly. I had to follow him to graves registration and put him in the bag myself. I couldn't let go of him. It was something I had to do.

Usually the expectants had massive head injuries. They were practically gone, they couldn't communicate with you. You were supposed to clean them up, call the chaplain. You did all that stuff, I guess, to make you feel as though you were helping them. To preserve their lives, you would've had to put them on a respirator and evac them to a neuro facility, which in our case would have been all the way to Da Nang, which was hours, miles away. I was an operating room nurse, but when there was a mass-cal, since there were only 12 of us, we'd be called into triage to work there. After that, I'd follow them into the operating room and help do the surgery. A lot of the shrapnel extractions we'd do ourselves, and a lot of the closures too. The docs would say, "Why don't you close? I got this next case in the next room." You didn't have to worry about it too much, if you got into trouble he'd be right there next door.

We wanted to save everyone. We had a lot of ARVNs (Army of the Republic of Vietnam), we called them "Marvin the ARVN." We tried to take care of the Americans first, but we also had to take care of whoever needed care—period, whether he was a Vietnamese, a POW, or whatever. In fact, when we tried to save Cliff, they brought in the Vietnamese who had laid the mine. He had an amputation. He was bleeding badly and had to be treated right away. And we saved him. I guess in my heart I felt angry about what happened.

We were short on anesthesia and supplies. And we were giving anesthesia to this POW, which made me angry because I thought, "What if—what happens if someone comes in like Cliff and we don't have any anesthesia left because we gave it all to this POW?" Again, because I was very strongly Catholic, as soon as I heard myself thinking this, I thought, "God, how can you think that? The tables could be turned, and what if it was Cliff in the POW's place, and how would I feel if he received no anesthesia simply because he was an enemy?" First of all, it shocked me and embarrassed me. It made me think, "Gosh, I'm losing my values, what's happened to me?" I had been taught in nursing school to save everybody regardless of race, creed, color, ethnic background, whatever. Life is life. But suddenly I wasn't thinking that anymore. I was thinking, "I'm American, and they're the enemy. Kill the enemy and save the American."

Before I went to Vietnam, I was kind of bubbly, excited about life. I haven't changed that much really, I'm still that way. But back then, suddenly, I began questioning things, wondering about what we were doing there. I remember talking with the chaplain, saying, "What are we doing? For what purpose are we here?" We were training Vietnamese helicopter pilots to go out and pick up their wounded and take them to their hospitals. And we treated plenty of them at our hospitals, too. Yet when we'd call up and say, "We got a wounded soldier in Timbuktu," they'd say, "It's five o'clock and we don't fly at night." We had soldiers in the hospital shot by 10-year-old boys and girls. We had women who'd invite GIs to dinner—nice women—and they'd have someone come out from behind a curtain and shoot them all down dead. I mean, what kind of war was this?

The chaplain told me, "Hey Jacque, you can't condemn the American government. We can't say the American government is wrong to put us in this position here. We can't say, because there is so much we don't know." It was good advice at the time, it really helped me. I was thinking, "Here I am judging, and I'm saying what the heck are we doing here, look at all these lives lost, all these young boys and for what? And who am I to judge that? There has to be a reason." I guess I'm still trying to hold on to that belief, even though people laugh at me when I say it. They think I'm living in a dream world because I'm hoping there was a good reason.

I didn't really have much time to worry about right and wrong back then, because during these mass-cals we'd be up for 36 hours at a stretch. Nobody wanted to quit until the last surgery case was stabilized. By that time, we were emotionally and physically numb. You couldn't see clearly, you couldn't react. Sounds were distant. We kind of policed each other. When we saw each other reacting strangely or slowly, we'd say, "Hey, Jacque, get some sleep, someone will cover, go get some sleep." That's how close we were. That's how we coped with stress.

You didn't have time to think about how unhappy you were. It was afterwards, when you couldn't go to sleep . . . here you were without sleep for 36 hours, lying in your bed expecting sleep to overwhelm you, but you couldn't fall asleep because you were so tensed and stressed from what you saw. I knew I had a problem the day I was with a nurse I was training who was going to replace someone else. I remember I had completed this amputation and I had the soldier's leg under my arm. I was holding the leg because I had to dress it up and give it to graves registration. They'd handle all the severed limbs in a respectful manner. They wouldn't just throw them in the garbage pile and burn them. They were specially labeled and handled the good old government way.

I remember this nurse came in and she was scheduled to take the place of another nurse. When she saw me, I went to greet her and I had this leg under my arm. She collapsed on the ground in a dead faint. I thought, "What could possibly be wrong with her?" There I was trying to figure out what's wrong with her, not realizing that here I had this leg with a combat boot still on and half this man's combat fatigue still on, blood dripping over the exposed end. And I had no idea this might bother her.

We had a lot of big parties, too. The Army had all these rules about fraternization, how officers couldn't fraternize with enlisted. In Quang Tri, we were just one big family. You didn't worry about who had an E-2 stripe or who had the colonel's insignia. I'm not saying we didn't have problems with officers and enlisted people or things like insubordination. But everybody partied together.

I never had a sexual relationship over there. You have to remember how Catholic I was. Dating, well, you'd walk around bunkers and talk about home. Every hooch had a bunker, so you'd bring a bottle of wine and he'd bring glasses and—this sounds gross, I guess— you'd sit and watch the B-52s bomb across the DMZ. It produced this northern lights effect. The sky would light up in different colors and you'd sit and watch the fireworks. I know it sounds strange, watching somebody's village get blown up. We didn't want to think about the lives being lost.

The grunts always knew where the female nurses were. They all knew that at the hospital there was a good chance of seeing a "round-eye." Once, during monsoon season, we received a dust off call saying there'd been a truck convoy ambush involving 40 or 50 guys. They were in bad shape but not far from the hospital, maybe seven or eight miles. We could stand on the tops of our bunkers and see flashes of light from where they were fighting the VC. One of these deuce-and-a-half trucks with a load of wounded came barreling up right into our triage area. Like I said, they all knew where the hospital was. The truck's canvas and wood back part were all on fire. Evidently they had just thrown the wounded in back and driven straight for us.

We were concerned about the truck, about getting it out of the way, but we were also trying to get to the wounded. There were two guys in the back, standing up. There was a third guy we couldn't see, and the first two were carrying him and shrieking at the top of their lungs. One was holding the upper part of his torso, under the arms, and the other held the legs. Their eyes were wild and they were screaming. I couldn't see what was wrong with the guy they were carrying. Everyone else on the truck was jumping off. We were shouting to these guys to get off too, that the truck was about to explode. We were screaming, "You're OK, you're at the hospital."

Two of the corpsmen got up in the truck, grabbing them to let go and get moving. The corpsmen literally had to pick them up and throw them off the truck. Once they were off, they sat down in a heap, still shrieking. It wasn't until then that I got a look at the wounded one. He didn't have a head. He must have been a buddy of theirs. The buddy system was very strong, and these two evidently weren't going to leave without their friend. We brought them to the docs and had them sedated. We didn't have any psychiatric facilities, so we got them evac'd to Da Nang. We never heard what happened to them.

After awhile in Vietnam, I guess I wasn't so young anymore. I was seeing things, doing things that I never imagined could happen to anyone. I had to do a lot of things on my own, making snap decisions that could end up saving someone or costing him his life. Like once, when I'd been there about seven months, they brought in this guy who'd been shot square in the face. It was the middle of the night and I was on duty with a medical corpsmen, no doctors around at all. They were sleeping, saving their strength. We got the call from dust off that this guy was coming in. Apparently he'd been shot by a sniper. Amazingly enough, he was conscious when they brought him in. As a matter of fact, he was sitting up on the stretcher. It was incredible.

His face was a huge hole, covered with blood. You couldn't see his eyes, his nose, or his mouth. There was no support for his jaw and his tongue was just hanging. You could hear the sound of blood gurgling as he took a breath, which meant he was taking blood into his lungs. We were afraid he'd aspirate. The corpsman was this older guy, over 40 anyway, an experienced sergeant. I took a look at this guy and knew we'd have to do a trach on him pretty fast. He couldn't hear us and we couldn't get him to lie down.

I told the sergeant, "We gotta call the doc in." He told me we didn't have time for that. We had to stabilize him with a trach and ship him out to Da Nang. I told the corpsman that the only time I'd ever done a trach was on a goat back in basic training at Fort Sam Houston. The corpsman said, "If you don't do it, he'll die." So he put my gloves on for me, and handed me the scalpel. I was shaking so badly I thought I'd cut his throat. I remember making the incision, and hearing him cough. The blood came out of the hole, he was coughing out everything he was breathing in. The drops flew into my eyes, spotting my contact lenses. After the blood finished spurting out, we slid the tube in. He laid back and I worried, "What's going on?"

But he was breathing. He didn't have to fight or struggle for breath anymore. I could see the air was escaping from the trach, just like it was supposed to. It was a beautiful feeling, believe me. We packed his face with four-by-fours and roller gauze to stop the bleeding. We told him what we were doing and he nodded his head. When they finally loaded him up for the trip to Da Nang, I was shaking pretty badly. The whole thing had taken less than 45 minutes, from the time dust off landed to the time we packed him off. We never did get his name.

But three months later, I was sitting in the mess hall in Da Nang, waiting to take a C–130 to Hong Kong for R&R. I'd been in country 10 months by then, and I was in the mess hall alone, drinking coffee and eating lunch, still in my fatigues. Somebody tapped me on the shoulder. I remember turning around. You have to remember, I was used to guys being friendly. I saw this guy standing there in hospital pajamas, the green-gray kind with the medical corps insignia on it. He had blond hair on the sides, bald on top. His face was a mass of scars, and you could see the outline of a jaw and chin. He had lips and a mouth, but no teeth. He looked like he had been badly burned, with a lot of scar tissue. You couldn't really tell where his lips began and the scar tissue ended.

The rest of his body was fine, and he could talk. "Do you remember me?" I was used to that, too, people coming up to me and saying, "Hey, I drove that tank by you the other day. . . . " Then he pointed to his trach scar and I said, "You can't be the same guy." He said something like, "I'll never forget you." I asked him how he knew who I was, because, I mean, there had been nothing left of his face. Apparently, the shot had flipped this skin flap up over his eyes so he could still see through the corners. I couldn't believe it. They called my flight right then, so I started saying a hasty goodbye. He mumbled something about how they had taken his ribs from his ribcage and artificially made a jawbone, and reconstructed portions of his face, taking skin from the lower legs, the buttocks.

Well, they began calling my name over the loud speaker. I remember giving him a big hug, saying I wished I had more time to talk to him. I wanted to learn his name, but I don't think he ever said it. I wanted to go back to the hospital and tell the others, "Hey, you remember what's-his-name? He's from Arkansas and he's doing fine." We always wanted to put names to faces, but we rarely got a chance to do it. You kept believing that everyone who left the hospital actually lived. When you found out someone actually had survived, it helped staff morale.

I came back home on a Friday, on a Pan American flight that landed in Seattle. I remember how we were told not to wear our uniforms, not to go out into the streets with our uniforms on. That made us feel worthless. There was no welcome home, not even from the Army people who processed your papers to terminate your time in the service. That was something. I felt like I had just lost my best friend. I decided to fly home to upstate New York in my uniform anyway. Nobody said anything. There were no dirty looks or comments. I was kind of excited. I wanted to say to people, "I just got back from Vietnam." Nobody cared. When I got home, my parents had a big banner strung up across the garage, "Welcome Home, Jacque." But that was about it. My parents were proud of me, of course. But other civilians? "Oh, you were in Vietnam? That's right, I remember reading something in the newspaper about you going there. That's nice." And then they'd go on talking about something else.

You were hungry to talk about it. You wanted so badly to say, "Gee, don't you want to hear about what's going on there, and what we did, and how proud you should be of your soldiers and your nurses and your doctors?" I expected them to be waiting there, waving the flag. I remember all those films of World War II, with the tape that flew from the buildings in New York City, the motorcades. Of course, I had my mother. My mom was always willing to listen, but of course she couldn't understand it when I started talking about "frag wounds" or "claymore mines." There was no way she could.

The first six months at home, I just wanted to go back to Vietnam. I wanted to go back to where I was needed, where I felt important. The first job I took was in San Francisco. It was awful. Nobody cared who I was. I remember the trouble I got into because I was doing more than a nurse was supposed to do. I got in trouble because I was a "mini-doctor." They kept saying, "You're acting like you're a doctor! You're doing all these things a doctor is supposed to do. What's the big idea? You're a nurse, not a doctor." And I thought, how can I forget all the stuff I learned—putting in chest tubes, doing trachs. True, doctors only do that, but how do you prevent yourself from doing things that came automatically to you for 18 months? How do you stop the wheels, and become the kind of nurse you were before you left?

I was completely different. Even my parents didn't recognize me as the immature little girl who left Albion, New York, just out of nursing school. San Francisco was a bomb, and there wasn't an Army post for miles around Albion. So that's why I came back to San Antonio. All my friends were back in and around Fort Sam Houston, so I just naturally gravitated back toward my network. I came to San Antonio in 1974 to get my B.S. in nursing from Incarnate Word College. The best thing I did was to get into the reserve unit there. That's where I met my husband. It gave me a chance to share my feelings with other Vietnam veterans. It kept me in touch with Army life, the good things and the bad. It was like a family.

On weekends at North Fort Hood, we really do sit around the campfire and talk about 'Nam, about what we as reservists can do to be better prepared than we were back there. If there is another Vietnam-type war, God forbid, I just know I'd want to be part of it. I couldn't sit on the sidelines. We usually just talk about these things among ourselves. I think the reason a lot of people are hesitant to talk about it is that they don't know anyone who wants to listen. A lot of people don't want to hear those kinds of stories. A lot of people just want to forget that time altogether. I don't know why. I guess I'm just not like that.

I'm not saying you don't pay a price for your memories. Last year, I had an intense flashback while flying on a Huey (helicopter) around North Fort Hood. It was the last day of this reserve unit exercise and I was invited on this tour of the area. We were flying a dust off, a medevac helicopter, just like the ones we had back then. It was my first time up in a helicopter since. I thought "Gee, this is going to be great." One of the other nurses said to me, "Are you sure you want to do this? You're pretty tired." I brushed her aside, "No problem." We sat in back in seats strapped in next to where they held the litters. I was sitting in the seat, the helicopter was reving up . . . I don't know how to describe it. It was like a slide show, one of the old-fashioned kind where you go through this quick sequence . . . flick, flick, flick . . . now I know where they got the term flashback.

At first, it was as though I was daydreaming. What scared me to death was that I couldn't turn it off. I couldn't control my mind. The cow grazing in the field became a water buffalo. Fields marked off and cross-sectioned became cemeteries. We flew over this tent, it was the 114th (reserve hospital unit) and suddenly it became the 18th surg. I was scared. All I could do was grasp the hand of this friend of mine. We couldn't talk above the helicopter roar. I just started to cry, I couldn't control myself. I saw blood coming down onto the windshield and the wiper blades swishing over it. There was blood on the floor, all over the passenger area where we were sitting. The stretchers clicked into place had bodies on top of them. I was crying. The nurse next to me kept shouting about whether I was all right. My contacts were swimming around, I wanted the ride to end. I could see why GIs felt scared . . . I couldn't just turn around and open up to the nurse sitting next to me. How could you explain something like that?

I had had a flashback or two before, but the difference was I could control them. Even when the nurse started shaking me, I couldn't turn it off. I just looked past her toward the racks in the helicopter, with bodies on stretchers, body bags on the floor, blood everywhere. When we landed, everyone saw I was visibly upset. The pilot came over to see if I was OK. The only thing I could say was, "It brought back a lot of memories." How could I explain my feelings to these people at North Fort Hood. A lot of them were too young to remember Vietnam as anything more than some dim kind of image on the nightly news. I was scared to death, because all these feelings were brought back that I never knew I had.

I still try to think of the good memories from Vietnam, the people we were able to save. A flashback has certain negative connotations. It's a flashback when they can't think of another way of explaining it. I guess I'm lucky it took 14 years for it to hit me like that. The one positive thing I can say about it is that it felt awfully good to come back and hover down to that red cross on the top of the tent. It felt good to come home.

Lorraine Boudreau

We called the big influxes of casualties "mass-cals," short for "mass casualty situation." The biggest mass-cal I ever saw was on my first tour at the 93rd evac in Long Binh. It was the first and the worst. I think I'd only been there three, four months. I remember the hospital wasn't even completed yet. It was early in the tour because the engineers were still putting the Quonset huts over us. It would have been December. There was a big push with the 1st Division and the 173rd Airborne Division. They had sustained massive casualties. They were bringing casualties not only to us at the 93rd, but if necessary they were flying them into Saigon—the 3rd Field there got some.

Two Chinooks landed on our helipad. A Chinook is equipped to handle 20 litters and 20 ambulatory cases, but somehow we ended up with 70 patients—the worst I've ever seen. The main problem we had was in the triage area, mostly because we were limited to how many people could work there. The doctors went from one litter to the next to determine which patients needed to go to the OR immediately. I can't remember how many operating rooms we had going at the time. I don't think we had our full complement of six; it was probably more like four. I remember the doctors becoming really

Lorraine Boudreau served two tours in Vietnam: the first in 1965–1966 at the 93rd Evacuation Hospital at Long Binh; the second in 1969–1970 at the 312th and 91st Evacuation Hospitals at Chu Lai. Born in West Warwick, Rhode Island, in 1943, she is currently a nurse researcher at the VA hospital in Kerrville, Texas.

frustrated. They also were inexperienced as far as this type of mass-casualty, real-life thing. It wasn't easy trying to determine who went first. The majority needed to go, but we had to decide who was the most critical.

I was mostly checking to make sure the patients were breathing, that if life support measures needed initiating, it got done. We also gave patients tetanus shots. Their dressings needed to be reinforced because they were bleeding. We had patients on litters all over the place—fragmentation wounds of the torso and abdomen, wounds of the extremities. I remember one patient I found probably about two-and-a-half hours later, stuck behind a box—we were still unpacking. He had a shoulder wound. It was pretty fleshy, so there was nothing major that had been hit. He was perfectly fine and content to stay where he was. He told me he felt his buddies needed care before he did, and that if he really needed something he would have yelled out. We only found him by accident. That was a bad situation.

I was trying to see which patients needed checking more frequently. I was doing triage in order to keep an eye on patients who needed more attention. As I remember, I got some patients geographically moved so I could consolidate patients who needed more attention into one area instead of trying to hop over bodies. I'd try to control some of the bleeding with new bandages, but that didn't always work. The expectant category was very rarely used. If the patient required extensive surgery, the patient got extensive surgery. The cases I remember that were "expectant" were the ones where there was no hope, such as extensive burns, say, over 80 percent of the body. These were the ones who were really crisp. They used a lot of armored personnel carriers . . . when an APC hits a land mine, you've got an inferno. I saw some 100 percent burn cases, these were expectant. One-hundred percent third degree is like a charcoal briquette. Probably one of the reasons I got out of surgical-type nursing is that I cannot stand the odor of burnt flesh. I find it extremely repulsive.

I remember feeling anxious, but it's like the adrenalin flows and you know you have to get through it. So you do it, and you think about it later. I don't really remember . . . there were some patients who did die before getting to the OR. There were also some patients who died en route, because we were putting those in body bags and stacking them on the side. In this push, over a couple of days, we treated over 200 patients. We worked 18–20 hours straight. When it was all over, I went to bed and tried to get some sleep. What I remember thinking is that I hoped this was not an everyday thing, because I couldn't see how one could manage with something like this happening everyday. I couldn't see how we could possibly manage because we were being tasked to the maximum. The number one problem was that we didn't have everything unpacked, and number two was that we were running out of supplies. At that time in '65, not only troops but also supplies were being brought in by ship. Half our equipment was being pilfered on the dock, so we never got it. The pilfering was being done not only by the black market, but also by combat units that needed medical supplies. We had to improvise a lot.

I remember one night on my first tour I was on duty in the triage area and we had 16 Vietnamese civilian casualties come in with napalm wounds. Seven or eight of them were children, and when I say children we're looking at age 11 or under. We did take care of civilian casualties, especially ones that we injured. This was a village not all that far from the hospital, 10 miles or so. They brought these civilians in, and out of the 16, 11 or 12 died. The skin turns white and peels right off. There is some flame, but mostly it's the chemical that just eats the skin away. It was almost like a powdery white sulphur type of thing—just awful. We were not all that well equipped to deal with civilian casualties. We needed the space for Americans. Basically what we did with the Vietnamese casualties was patch them up and send them off to the provincial hospital. If they were critical, they did not survive.

Incidents like this helped form a feeling that this was all a bunch of nonsense. We shoot them up, burn them up, and then we take care of them. It wasn't that I was disillusioned. I'd say I felt more confused. I was 22 years old and I knew nothing about the concept of war. I'd seen all the John Wayne movies, but John Wayne and the real thing are a world apart. I remember an overwhelming feeling of "What is this all about?" It didn't make any sense to me. I wasn't anti-Vietnam, but there was a certain confusion as it began registering in my mind that "these things really do happen." You read about these things, but it doesn't really register until you see it. At the hospital, they justified bombing small villages on the grounds that they were loaded with VC, which was true. The napalm isn't just marked with "VC Charlie" on it. There's going to be a lot of civilian casualties in a situation like that. I just thought it was an absolute waste of people's lives. I mean, war's stupid to begin with.

When I returned to Vietnam in 1969 things had changed dramatically. We weren't waging war out of a suitcase anymore. Our presence in Vietnam was pretty well established, but by the same token, our naiveté about the war was now completely gone. By 1969, for instance, fragging was becoming something that . . . I won't say it was routine, but it did happen a number of times. Fragging basically is our guys shooting at our guys. I remember that as soon as I got back in country, I called the husband of a friend of mine. He was a full colonel, and just several days before he'd been shot by one of his men. We had problems with fragging in the enlisted quarters. We had one case where a Marine threw a grenade in his barracks. You had a bunch of guys playing cards, and this one Marine throws a grenade and the thing went off. He killed two of his buddies and wounded the rest of them, maybe three or four, including himself. I gather he was loaded on drugs when he did it. They brought him in, put him on armed guard, not because he was going to go any place, but because they had to protect him from someone else coming in and finishing him off.

They brought one guy in once . . . I'll never forget this. I was working recovery room at the time. We were not all that busy. They had called me to tell me they had an expectant patient. He had a gunshot wound to the head; he was totally comatose. They had put a trach in and I believe he did have an IV going, more for aesthetic reasons than for ethical purposes, because it wasn't going to do anything. I couldn't even understand why they bothered to do the tracheostomy. He was evaluated by the doctor in the triage area and there was absolutely nothing that could be done for him, but he was still breathing. You have to remember these guys were healthy guys. Even with a gunshot wound to the head, if it hadn't hit the back of the brain and wiped out the respiratory center right away, there was no reason why he couldn't hang on for awhile. The bullet had made absolute mush of his brain. So anyway, I had him in the back of the

Quonset behind the screen. I knew he was expectant, and I went back there periodically to suction his tracheostomy out. And I remember I'd repack the dressing on his head because brain tissue was seeping out and running down the side of his face. He probably was an E-5, a buck sergeant. I found myself looking in his wallet to see if he had any pictures in his pockets. I wanted to know who he was. It doesn't really make a difference if you see a hundred casualties, this was another human being and I was interested in knowing more about him. We had some other casualties who were recovering after surgery, and they don't need to see someone dying while they're recovering. That's why he was behind the screen. My feeling was that one of the worst things that can happen to anybody is dying alone. Despite the fact that he was unconscious, comatose, he shouldn't die alone. He was still an individual. I found a picture of what appeared to be his wife and his child, a boy about two or three.

I think I felt the aloneness of it. Here was this American soldier, by himself, dying in this idiotic place. What was different about this one was that I had the time to think about it. If I had 20 people in my recovery room, I wouldn't have had the time to think about it. This time I did. I remember him rather vividly, like I remember the 18-year-old boy who died of malaria. I don't know how I ended up on the medical ward, but there I was, and one of the patients was dying of malaria and I held him as he died. Anopheles mosquitoes were rampant at the time, and you could still get malaria even if you were taking anti-malaria medication. You kind of took your chances. He had been there a week, maybe less than that. I remember talking to him. He was so sick. According to his chart, his prognosis was zero. His fever ran 105–106 degrees, even with a blanket, ice, and an alcohol bath. It was frying his brain. If someone was dying, if I had the time, I'd stay with him. No one should die alone. He was 18 years old. You go away, you're halfway around the world, you're fighting a stupid war, and you end up dying of malaria. You know, 18 years old. Let's face it. He didn't even get started in life.

Sharon Lane was another case. She was the only nurse to be killed on the ground by direct enemy fire. I knew her. In fact, I'd been eating dinner with her the night before. She was working the prisoner ward. Can you imagine the idiocy of that? This nurse comes over there to do what she'd been trained to do, and she ends up getting killed, on a Vietnamese prisoner ward. I remember that made me terribly angry. We weren't close friends. She was kind of a withdrawn person to begin with. I knew her as one of the LTs (lieutenants) working on the unit. The day before she died she was eating alone in the mess hall. When I got there, it was pretty much empty. So I just sat down and chit-chatted with her. I can't even remember what we talked about. And then the following morning she was killed.

Around that time I was tasked with taking over that ward. We had a new chief nurse, a colonel, who called me in her office to tell me she had a "special assignment" for me, the typical line. I remember asking her, "Colonel, I know what you're going to tell me. Why me?" I wasn't thrilled at this golden opportunity to take care of Vietnamese prisoners. But what are you going to do when you're a captain and the colonel tells you to do something? That was an interim period, I was still running the orthopedic ward and being oriented toward the Vietnamese ward. The VC I had no feeling for, these were first class, A-1, uptown bastards. Seeing what they did to the Vietnamese civilians with their tortures . . . all I had were feelings of hate.

The North Vietnamese, they were pretty nice folks. They were farmers and fishermen, pretty nice patients, receptive to the care. The VC would try to sabotage any care you'd give them just to be ornery. The North Viets actually turned out to be pretty cooperative and helpful. For one thing, they appreciated what you were doing for them, and if you found one who could speak a little English, he'd help you out. We had communications problems all the time.

I had some real problems with the other LTs. They weren't too happy with taking care of POWs either. The ward master and I were the only two people who were really permanent. We would not rotate off that unit. But the LTs would. They would rotate after about every three months they spent with me. Some of them treated the patients pretty miserably. I found one nurse kicking a prisoner in the shower one morning. Evidently this VC was not being very cooperative with having a shower, and he just sat down on the cement. Just as I walked in, one of the LTs gave him a quick kick in the butt with a combat boot. And at that point I just got the LT out of the shower area and out into the courtyard to have a cup of coffee while I dealt with the prisoner. I got a towel and ushered him back to bed. I guess I was trying to bury the feelings that I had, because I wasn't very happy with the POWs either.

I ended up spending more and more time on the unit. I began to feel more exhausted with work and the whole situation. There were these holes in the wall from that rocket attack that killed Sharon, and these served as constant reminders to me that I wasn't going home anytime soon. The ward was in a Quonset hut made of tin, and there were some odd gapping holes of various sizes from the rocket fragmentation. And we kept putting posters over the walls, mostly from magazines like *Holiday*. We had everything: scenes of Tahiti and I think we even had some Alaskan pictures. All these reminders of places other than Vietnam, just to cover the holes. And I saw them everyday. Being there in Vietnam was becoming a drain.

There were a lot of wounded coming in, especially Vietnamese casualties. We always had a massive turnover and we were always short of beds. There were times when we would end up putting two and three kids in the same bed. We had a lot of children and some of them were pretty badly wounded . . . traumatic amputations. We were also getting some of the casualties from the VC going through the villages doing their numbers on kids—things like chopping a foot off of a three-month-old baby. We had more casualties than we could take care of. And there were times when we sent people to the provincial hospital knowing full well they would not survive. But we had no choice.

I don't know if Sharon's death was a breaking point, but it sure was an impact point. Because I know after that I began to get scared. There was a time when I was doing a spin as the night supervisor for the whole hospital. I'd walk up and down the ramp making my rounds. And usually around three, four o'clock in the morning, I'd go back to the nursing office and pick up my jacket and helmet, just to make sure. And, I was scared. I really was scared knowing full well that it could happen again. I didn't want to die. I sure didn't. My feeling was that if you're number is up, you're going to go. But if you can do things to not put yourself into a situation where you help it along, then that's preferable. I'm a survivalist and always have been. I think that this is what has helped me through all these bad times— the willingness that "By God, I'm going to survive." I guess

Sharon's death made me look at my own vulnerability. I could have been killed too. Had that rocket waited 30 more minutes, I would have been on duty there. It was a sad situation but fortunately more people were not killed.

That was not the first rocket attack suffered on the unit. I remember one in particular. It must have been about 10:30 in the morning. The Viet Cong had bamboo tripods, so they weren't too accurate with these rockets. And all of a sudden we heard a couple of rockets hit the beach down the road. Then one hit inside the compound, but didn't hit any structure. I remember that day I had mixed some IV solution and I was halfway to the refrigerator to put two bottles inside when this rocket went off. And for a split second I didn't quite know what to do. I knew I needed to get on the cement, but I wasn't sure what I was going to do with my IV bottles. So I dove with them and broke one. Probably I should have just thrown them down and hit the dirt. I was scared and I didn't know which way to turn.

During the '69 moratorium, some of my corpsmen came in wearing black armbands. I made the decision that if the hospital commander wanted them to take the armbands off, he could come down and do it himself. By this time I was wondering "what are we doing?" We hadn't made any progress. Progress was measured not in terms of territory but in body counts. The VC had their body counts too. They had spies counting the bodies when they were hauled off the helicopters.

My answer to all this was that I drank myself silly. Everyone had their way of coping. You used those things to survive. You had booze, you had drugs, you had sex. I just wasn't into carousing around. A number of nurses did that—I can't say a lot. That was never my thing. I drank. I may have come on duty with a bad hangover, but I never drank on duty. I never drank alone. It was always with my friend Ginny, the Red Cross worker who lived in the next room. We developed a friendship sitting on the porch passing the bottle. We brought out patio furniture and ice, and there was always a bottle of Chivas on the table. It was 20-year-old Chivas, nothing but the best. I did a fair amount of drinking. But you can only drink so much until fatigue takes over, and you've got to get some sleep. There were always parties to go to. I had developed friendships with some of the outside units in the Americal Division. I knew the commander of the medevac unit and the S&T Battalion, and toward the end I went to some parties with the assistant division commander who was a brigadier general. The only group I wasn't crazy about was the Marines. They were macho! And they were kind of pushy—they don't like taking no for an answer. I remember this general, he was a nice, nice man. We talked a lot about the war and he helped me.

I didn't totally withdraw. I may have done a lot of drinking, but I wasn't socially withdrawn. The alcohol served as an anesthetic for me. I'd just phase out so I didn't think about Vietnam. Still, I knew full well that I'd get up in the morning and go through it all again. In the evenings it was just like time to blot it all out. Those evenings out on the porch, there'd always be music. Somebody would have a stereo on, stereos were going on all the time. Ginny would be chatting away about anything and everything. The content of conversations had nothing to do with what was going on as far as the war. It was always talking about something else—going on R&R, who's been where, different places in the country with different people. But we never talked about what was going on. Nobody ever did. We talked about everything else except what was going on. Nobody wanted to talk about it. And that's been an ongoing thing with Vietnam veterans. Nobody talks about it. We didn't talk about it then. No one ever really got into feelings. And my feeling is that God forbid we should ever have to do it again and end up going again. I know what I would do differently. I'd make sure I'd talk about what was going on inside me and try to develop a real strong support system. I feel strongly about that.

In the mornings I'd get up and I'd still be in 'Nam and I'd be tired. I was always tired. And I'd drag myself down to the shower and I'd get dressed and go to the mess hall and have coffee and breakfast. But I was tired. I guess I never realized just how tired I was till I went on R&R about a month-and-a-half before I came back. I was in Bangkok. I remember getting to the hotel and sighing, "Oh how nice, there's a bathtub." And after the bath, thinking, "I'll take a quick nap." This was about two o'clock in the afternoon. When I awoke, I looked at my watch and it said eight o'clock. But I wasn't sure what eight o'clock it was. I called down to the front desk and found out it was eight o'clock in the morning—the following morning. I had slept soundly from two o'clock in the afternoon to eight o'clock the following morning. That's how tired I was.

I was beginning to drag. I had to drag my whole body around. I was completely saturated. There was a guy I knew, an assistant battalion commander who was a major in the American Division. He came knocking on my door one Sunday morning when I had off. He was absolutely at odds with himself. His unit had just gone through a village and destroyed it. They went in looking for VC, and I guess they shot a lot of men, women, and children. It wasn't execution style. The one thing he did say is that they started shooting back, and you didn't know who was VC and who wasn't. He was distraught, and I talked to him for awhile and then I suggested that he go back over to division headquarters. And after he had left I felt somewhat guilty with sort of giving him the brush off. Why hadn't I spent more time listening to him? Because I didn't want to. I just didn't want to. I didn't want to deal with what he had to say. I didn't want to deal with somebody else's pain and frustration, because I couldn't even deal with my own.

Eventually, the day came when it was time for me to go home. It was January, blazing hot in Vietnam. But back in Rhode Island, it was bleak and pretty cold. I remember feeling terribly tired. I spent 30 days of leave at home with my family. A lot of that time was passed sitting in this one rocking chair in the kitchen looking out the window. All that was outside was the bleakness, and the snow, and the cold. I was home, but I had a feeling of isolation. That's when I really felt this terrible emptiness within myself.

In February, I was assigned to an Army hospital in Valley Forge, just outside of Philadelphia. The standing joke around Valley Forge was this big mural in the hospital portraying George Washington kneeling in the snow during the Revolutionary War. We said he was praying for his transfer out of Valley Forge. That's how everybody felt about it. I did not want to be there. It didn't take me long to figure out the war was still going on, even at Valley Forge. We were getting casualties right and left, just like Vietnam. I was assistant head nurse of ICU. I still drank a lot and I guess that was pushing me over.

I remember this one patient named Frank. He was about 19 or 20 years old. He had lost part of his face, one of his cheeks, half his chin . . . severe maxillofacial wounds. Half his tongue was gone, so he had difficulty communicating. When he was in Japan he had developed a stress ulcer, so he had a partial gastrectomy. He was on IV hyperalimentation. He wanted to die. His family was coming to see him on a certain day, and he did not want to see them at all. I remember I was there when his family arrived. He was totally withdrawn, trying to hide under the covers. The visit was a disaster. He had no interest in trying to get any better. He just wanted to die. Finally, I just lost my temper with him. Here we are and I'm doing the best I can to provide him nursing care, and he wants to die! I got so pissed off one day, I went in there and slammed the door shut and just absolutely unleashed on him. I said something like, "Who the hell do you think you are?" I just ventilated my feelings on him, that here he's been given the best of care, that here he's survived, that despite everything he's still alive, and that he was really being a first class shit. I remember saying, "If you don't care about yourself, why should anyone else?" After that he started getting better. There was a turning point, and I guess my tongue lashing had something to do with it. I was very frustrated. I felt bad for saying what I said to him, but when I saw he was making progress after that I figured, well, it was worth it. I still have strong feelings of guilt about that. It's just not something you do.

I knew I just couldn't deal with intensive care situations anymore. Patients were dying and I had had enough. Enough is enough is enough. And I knew I was getting more and more depressed. It was getting harder and harder to go to work. I talked to the education and training person at the hospital, and she suggested I go talk to the chief nurse about a different assignment. So I went to the chief nurse, told her I had had enough of death and dying. The one thing I didn't want to do, I did. I felt so bad and all of a sudden tears started coming down, and the colonel just leaned over and said, "We'll have none of that, Captain." It really does wonders for one's morale. "No, you will not be reassigned. You were specifically chosen for this particular position."

So there I was, I couldn't get off the intensive care unit. So I decided, "Well, this is ridiculous." Here I am feeling worse and worse, drinking more and more. All I was doing was going to work, coming home, drinking scotch at night, going to bed, and going to work in the morning. This was a lot of lonely drinking. Valley Forge is way to hell and gone, removed from everything. I was socially withdrawn, barely making it to work. I just didn't have the energy.

There were several active-duty folks (nurses and occupational therapists) who were living in my apartment complex who were having Friday night gatherings. We were bringing our knitting and crocheting. The apartment changed every Friday, and whoever was hosting would provide cake and coffee. And I remember one night, here I was crocheting this afghan, and all of a sudden I remember thinking, "Why am I doing this?" I mean, it was like an old maid sewing circle. That's exactly what it was. I said I can't deal with this, either. I remember I excused myself to go home. The worst part of it was that as bad as I felt, as depressed as I was, I was trying to get someone to listen to me, and that was the hardest thing. Nobody wanted to hear it!

I decided this is stupid, someone's got to listen to what I have to say. And having had psychiatry in nursing school, I knew what the symptoms of depression were and I felt that I was getting to be in not too good shape. I made an appointment with an Army psychiatrist, and after 20 minutes of talking he told me, "All right, come back when you feel better." I said, "No, wait a minute. This doesn't make sense." So I made an appointment with the chief of psychiatry. I figured I might as well talk to the boss and find out what he had to say. He talked to me for about an hour and thought I could benefit from some therapy. But he said that he didn't have any time and I asked him why, and he said, "I have too many patients." So I asked him what he meant, what kind of patients and he said "dependent wives"—the wives of male officers. I said, "Well, let me get this straight, I'm the one who's active-duty military," and he said he was sorry about that. So then his secretary realized what was going on. She gave me a business card of a doctor in King of Prussia who had just gotten out of the Army. "Maybe he'll listen to you."

I started going to see this psychiatrist a couple times a week. He charged me $35 a visit. I was paying out of my own pocket. He didn't want to hear what I wanted to say about 'Nam. He was

Freudian-oriented and he wanted to go back to childhood, and I told him that's not what I needed to deal with. What I needed to deal with was what was going on right now. Some crisis intervention was what I needed. But he wasn't interested, he didn't want to deal with that.

I had been to a party one night. I was driving home, and all I remember is that I stopped the car because I knew I didn't want to go home to the empty apartment, and I knew I didn't want to go to work. A friend of mine had left after I did, and she saw my car so she pulled over. I was just sitting in the car, just absolutely crying my heart out. She said, "Jesus. I think it's time you get some help." She took me to the outpatient clinic. We found a doctor who was somewhat sympathetic. He decided I couldn't go back on active duty. So they admitted me. I figured I couldn't get any worse. I was admitted to Valley Forge and within a week I was transferred to Walter Reed. They wanted me out of Valley Forge. Soon after, I came back to return to work, and I had the same chief nurse. In my absence, she had given me a bad evaluation. She had really drug me through the coals, writing how I was uncooperative, on and on and on; and then they gave me the assignment as chief nurse of the recovery room. I asked, "If you think I'm incompetent and in-effective, why make me head nurse of the recovery room?" And they said, "Don't pay any attention to that. You're going to be head nurse." So I decided screw this business, I went back to Walter Reed. I didn't want to work anymore. I couldn't deal with it.

I had post-traumatic stress disorder, only they didn't call it that back then. I don't think I really fell over the brink. A part of me was well and normal and functioning, but the other part of me was ex-hausted and saying, "Enough is enough." Since it was obvious I couldn't deal with it anymore, and since I couldn't get anybody to deal with it for me, someone had to take the bull by the horns and make a decision. And I think it was the healthy part of me that made the decision, that said: "OK Lorraine, this is it. Now in order for you to survive you have got to pull it together." I guess my way of pulling it together was falling apart. In the military, you're on duty or you're not on duty. And if you're not on duty, you're either on leave or you are sick. I think that was my out—that's how the doctor came to decide that in order to get me out of this particular environment, the only thing he could do was admit me. I think basically my problem

was that I was terribly exhausted. I had had war more than I could
tolerate anymore. I was completely saturated with it. And yet, there
was no way I could deal with it because I couldn't deal with myself.
And so putting me at Walter Reed was one way of getting me out of
the environment. But I never lost contact with reality. I knew what
was going on, but a part of me just couldn't deal with it. Religion has
played a certain role in my life, and I guess at that time God kind of
took over a bit for awhile. And God had me get in gear. So I think
between God and myself we kind of pulled it out.

Gradually, things began settling down at Walter Reed. I had my
once-a-week session with the psychiatrist, and I was in a couple of
joint therapy groups. The rest of the time I went bowling and swimming, that sort of stuff. Around the time all this was happening, I
was also taking my SATs and applying to the University of Virginia
for an undergraduate degree program in nursing. That was the
healthy side of me in operation. I was just waiting for the time of my
release from active duty, June of 1971. I finally got released and put
my stuff in storage, because by this time I knew I was moving to
Charlottesville.

Once I got myself in gear, amazingly enough, I did pretty well.
The only time I ever had a problem from then on was when something happened that triggered a flashback. For instance, I was doing
this special project at UVA, making a training film. I needed to film
a sequence in a hospital recovery room, and after getting permission
I found myself standing at a desk watching patients being wheeled
in and out of the OR. All of a sudden I was not at UVA. I was back
in 'Nam seeing patients being wheeled back and forth. It didn't last
that long. Right away it startled me, maybe for a minute or so. What
I was seeing was bloody wounds, when in reality what was being
wheeled in were hernias and such. I hadn't had a flashback up until
that time.

I was watching TV when Vietnam fell in 1975. Around that time,
I started having some serious nightmares. They concerned the
"mass-cal" situations, helicopters, triage, you name it. In these
dreams, I was constantly being overwhelmed. There was always too
much. I'd wake up in the middle of the night in a cold sweat, hyper-
ventilating. In California, I was taking the command and general
staff course at Edwards Air Force Base as part of my reserve obliga-

tion, and I remember a couple of times ending up on the floor from nightmares. Not rocket nightmares, just lots of people and being chased. There was always someone with a gun chasing me, and I could never see his face. I went to a counselor to help me over that.

I've had other flashbacks or times when I felt ill at ease and was able to trace it back to Vietnam. One example is the day the space shuttle exploded. Watching that on television at work, the gut level feeling that I had and the sadness that I felt was similar to what I went through in Vietnam. And I hadn't felt that in a long, long time. Another time I had a flashback was at North Fort Hood on reserve duty. The third day of this field exercise on chemical casualty care, it happened in the back of a deuce-and-a-half (truck). We went over the hill after we left the garrison area, and I started looking out the back. I saw the terrain and then the field hospitals and the tents and the red crosses. And for I don't know how long I wasn't at Fort Hood anymore. I was in the back of a deuce-and-a-half in Vietnam. I was seeing jungle instead of that Central Texas brush. I had a very sick gut-level feeling. And then I snapped back, and I realized what was going on. During the second week when I was doing the night shift and monitoring what was going on out there in the field, I came back to the garrison in the morning to try and get some sleep. But I couldn't, because the Huey helicopters flying mock casualties in and out of the hospital were driving me nuts. These were the same helicopters that brought our casualties to us in Vietnam. There was one point where I felt as though if they didn't stop I was going to absolutely scream. All in all though, the reserves proved to be a good way for me to keep in touch with my military experience. I can deal with the Army. It's Vietnam that was the problem. I still believe in this country and its defense. I think Vietnam was a mistake.

For women, for nurses in particular, it was a different war. There was a conflict of values. On the one hand you're indoctrinated; you're supposed to be caring. There's the Florence Nightingale pledge to heal the sick. With wounded guys, especially the 19 and 20 year olds, you were many things. You represented their girl-friends, their wives, their mothers. But, on the other hand, there was a sense of helplessness. You just couldn't do anything for the soldier with his brains pouring out or a malaria patient who dies in your arms. It becomes overwhelming, so you try to depersonalize it.

But no matter what you do, you can never shut it out altogether. To rid ourselves of our guilt, at least some of us have become workaholics, successaholics. We have a drive to succeed. I got out of the Army and got a bachelor's and master's in nursing. It's not an ego thing. I was just trying to compensate, trying to feel better about myself. What I didn't realize until recently was that I was carrying all this around inside me . . . and I never had a chance to talk about it.

Lois Johns

My orders to Vietnam came through two to three weeks before my 40th birthday. Great way to become 40. It wasn't anything that earth-shattering, just part of the job. When you're in the military, you learn to go where you're sent. You can complain now and then; but when it comes to a war situation, you're not going to complain too much. Each one of us had a job to do, and the professional nurse in the Army is trained to go where the men are and to take care of wounded and sick individuals. The orders came through in April of '67. I was at the University of Utah finishing up my doctorate in educational psychology, on Army time and Army pay. I was a major at the time. I knew a new assignment was coming because I had been out to the American Nurses' Association Convention in San Francisco the previous year. And while I was there I spoke with some of the people from the Army Nurse Corps, one of whom told me to hurry along and finish my degree so that I could be reassigned somewhere. I'd already been in school three years, and for every year you went to school, you owed the Army two. So there was a certain definite incentive to get the degree.

At first, the rumor was that I was going to Korea. So I told my

---

Lois A. Johns served in 1967–68 as chief nurse of the 629th Medical Detachment (Renal) attached to the 3rd Field Hospital based in Saigon. Born in Cleveland in 1927, she went on active duty in the Army in 1960, and retired as a full colonel in 1980. She is a nursing research consultant and lives in San Antonio. She is also a Fellow of the American Academy of Nursing.

family I might go to Korea when I left school. When the orders arrived, naturally enough I thought it was Korea. I opened it up and it was Vietnam. And my mother said to me on the phone, "You asked for that." And I said "No, I didn't ask for it, but everybody else is going so I presumed that I would logically go." The only thing about it was the first thing that is supposed to happen after you get a doctorate in the Army is that you're supposed to go on a "tour of utilization," where you get to use your new degree. Instead I went to Vietnam. But I have to admit I got to use my doctorate very definitely with the personnel who worked with me.

Although I had gotten my orders, I wasn't scheduled to go until the end of summer. I wasn't overly eager to go to Vietnam, but I wasn't overly eager to stay at home either. I had been on active duty at that point for seven years, and I had not been overseas. That's a long time to have been in the Army as a career person and not to have been overseas. In all honesty, I'd rather have gone to Vietnam for one year than to Europe for three. I'm not a European-oriented individual.

I had at least one thing going for me in Vietnam that most of the younger nurses didn't. I'd been around in the Army long enough to build up a support network. When I arrived, I found I already knew the chief nurse—I had worked with her at the Burn Unit at BAMC (Brooke Army Medical Center in San Antonio) in 1961. That's what I mean about the support network. Here I am going into a strange area, but I meet someone I know. When you're a lieutenant or a captain, it's us versus them. After major, you're a corporate member. So I had this support system which the majority of the lieutenants and captains did not have. They got out of nursing school and they had to adjust to the fact that they were graduates. Then they had to adjust to the fact that they were in the Army. Then they had to adjust to the fact that they were in Vietnam. They had an awful lot of adjusting to do within six months to a year of coming into the Army.

The prospect of being in Vietnam didn't upset me. I got more upset about Vietnam when I got there and I took a look at what was going on. I didn't get upset about my job, the work I had to do, or, for the most part, the people I had to work with. What upset me was the situation that I saw. I guess that my expectation had been that the people over there wanted us there. I was over there a relatively short period of time, like a month or so, when two of the nurses—who had been there longer—and I got a chance to leave the hospital compound in civilian clothes. I was introduced to the Saigon Zoo, which was a magnificent zoo at that time. Then we went to the central market in downtown Saigon. And we walked around the outside of it looking at all the different things that were there. Then we decided we would go inside the market area. All of a sudden all three of us stopped and looked at each other. We were being intensely hated. You could feel it. It wasn't just one person. We could feel that we were just somehow in a group where we were hated by the people who were around us. And we got out of there fast. About as fast as we could, we hunted up an exit and left. You really don't want to stay in that situation when you can feel it that intensely. We got outside and we talked about it. We left and then we went to one of the hotels and went up on the top of the roof and sat up there and had a drink and talked about it some more.

It was after that when I started to take a look around me. I found that I felt threatened. These people didn't want us there. What they wanted was peace, being able to do their thing, their way. And they really didn't want us over there. Of course, there *were* a lot of people that wanted us. The Vietnamese Army thought that we were great. The Vietnamese political situation needed our backing to be able to stay in power.

In the Far East everybody takes a little bit, but not a whole lot. Everybody gets a piece of the action. And that really didn't bother me, because I watched and I knew what was going on. But then I met the widow of a Vietnamese general. The general had been killed and she was allowed to live on the military compound in a house furnished by the Vietnamese government. She had two or maybe three of her daughters—anyway several daughters—in Paris studying. And they were going to stay in Paris. And she was discussing how she was going to get the son out of the country and into Paris to study. She was far more oriented toward France than toward the United States, which probably is understandable because the French were there a long time. Anyhow we got into this great discussion, and she talked about various things and I listened to her and I looked around her house. She had all these beautiful pieces in jade, magnificent sculptures of jade in red, and black, and blue. This is no

soapstone or anything, this is *jade* jade. I would say that she had
several hundred thousand dollars worth of jade in that house, and it
was clear her plan was that when her son left for France, she would
leave with him and take these pieces of jade with her.

Sometime later, she was in the hospital and she had these packages with her, and I found out at that point that she was the Vietnamese chairman for the World Vision group. The World Vision
group, in an effort to control some kind of eye problem, was sending
hog cholera vaccine to Vietnam. It had to be kept under refrigeration. It was supposed to be passed out to the farmers. But what was
going on was that this lady was appropriating the majority of it for
her hog farm. Her hogs were well taken care of. I don't know about
anybody else's. And she kept the vaccine in the refrigerators at the
hospital. The physicians allowed her to do this. The order came that
the chief would allow for the vaccine to be in our refrigerator until it
was time for it to be removed, and I got somewhat irritated with this
idea. The vaccine was supposed to be given out and she was apparently keeping the master share of it. I really didn't need marching
people in the United States to prove to me we had a problem in
Vietnam. I had the example of this woman.

There were a few other things of this nature. I made a tape to my
parents and told them that the Vietnamese didn't seem to want us
there. You know, I felt very strongly at that point—I had been there
about four months—that once we were gone that the Vietnamese
within six months or maybe a year would be communist. The communists would overrun the country whenever we would leave, because the people wanted peace.

I shared my quarters with the assistant chief nurse of the hospital,
which meant that I got an awful lot of input about what was going on
within the hospital with the different types of patients who came in.
We had a wide variety because we had patients transferred to us
from all over Vietnam. We kept them for awhile and then sent them
on to Japan. The longest we could hold patients was about 60 days.
Probably two-thirds of the injuries I saw were battlefield. One-third
were medical. We saw a lot of "swine fever" from soldiers swimming in ponds and swallowing water. Several went into renal failure.
We had five beds and two kidney machines. In the year I was there

we had 110 patients. That may not seem like a lot, but the difference was the amount of effort we put into it. We got to know our patients. The least amount of time I had a patient was 12 hours—a Montagnard tribesman who died.

The way the situation was with the Renal Unit, patients were injured, say, during a night attack or whatever. They had severe injuries and were being treated at another hospital, and they came to us when the doctors realized that they were into renal failure. They were sent to us maybe 24–48 hours after they were wounded. And we had a problem then of treating the kidney failure together with the injury. We were the only renal unit in the Army pattern and we took care of the patient 24 hours a day.

We used a fairly large amount of peritoneal dialysis. This was when you poured a couple of gallons, or maybe half a gallon, of fluid into the peritoneal cavity, let it sit for maybe 20 minutes to a half hour, whatever the physician dictated, and then let it all drain out. And there is a slow exchange there between the components within the blood and the components in the dialysate. And in that pattern, one hour of the regular use of a kidney machine is equal to say 24–36 hours of using peritoneal dialysis. Compared to other parts of the hospital, we didn't have a large number of patients, but we always had several patients at a time under this constant care. We were separate from the rest of the hospital in various ways. And all the work and the rest of it that we did was within our own little ward section that was blocked off, and of course the patient's viewpoint was that once you entered the kidney unit you weren't coming out again—alive. Well, when I was there, we carried a 56 percent, 55–56 percent, mortality rate. Among the surgical patients alone we had a 75 percent mortality rate. But among the medical patients it was 33 percent.

Anyhow the patient's attitude was that once you entered our room you weren't going to come back out. Now that rate was only for the year that I was there. Since we had these patients for a period of time, you got to know them awfully well. Now when we get to the time of the Tet offensive, the number of patients picked up. And we got busier and busier. When the Khe Sanh seige was on we treated about 10 or 11 Marines. We had one after another coming down from Khe Sanh with massive injuries. Renal failure wasn't the only thing. These guys had stepped on land mines, and it had blown both legs off as well as testicles. The whole perineal area was, you know . . . they really should have been dead, but they had gotten treatment in time before being brought to us.

I used to think, and still do, that in great part they were brought down not necessarily so the doctors could keep them alive—though that was part of the intent—but so they could see whether the artificial kidney would help at all. It wasn't experimentation, really. It was just that the physicians felt the need to know . . . they wanted to bring the patients down and try to see if they could save them with the use of a kidney. And my feeling was, and that of my personnel as we talked about it was . . . because several of them came and expressed things to me . . . that they really wished they hadn't brought those patients down. We sort of had a general feeling that the patients should have been left to die.

Florence Nightingale never said you had to save everybody. The biggest thing in medicine is "Do no harm!" And so, no harm was ever done. But the emphasis on keeping patients alive was not a good one to me. Physicians are taught in schools of medicine and nurses are taught in schools of nursing that you fight like the dickens to keep all patients alive. You know, everyone is going to get cured. There's only one small problem, it's not true. Everybody's still going to die. And sometimes you have to step back and let the individual die. I became very certain of that. I learned that in the Burn Unit in San Antonio the first time there. I learned it to a greater depth in Vietnam, because of some of the patients—the men from Khe Sanh who came down with such absolutely severe injuries.

We had this one young man come into our unit whose family knew the Secretary of State, Dean Rusk. The young man had not been in Vietnam too long when his unit had been attacked. He ran around and directed fire and got wounded. He was given a medal. In the hospital he was a paraplegic and went into renal failure. So we had him for a period of time. His brother was teaching English in Japan. Through Dean Rusk, the family arranged to get the younger brother sent to Vietnam. The brother came in and the wounded one started going downhill. On Christmas Eve, he was doing very poorly. He was seen by Bob Hope at midnight as well as General Westmoreland. They were making their rounds at the hospital before going to a Christmas Mass. After that, he seemed to do worse. We discussed it, those of us who were on duty, and we decided we really needed to keep him alive because someone shouldn't die on Christmas. We didn't think a family should get word that the young man would die on Christmas. You know, there was a M*A*S*H episode about this very thing, keeping a man alive on Christmas. I déjà vued tremendously on that. He continued to live for another two weeks or so.

I went back and looked at it from a psychologist's point of view. I couldn't decide who we had been treating on Christmas Eve, the family or ourselves. And then, over time, I regretted the fact that we had not let nature take its normal course. He became very confused, delirious, he lost a great deal of weight. He changed from what his brother knew to a totally different patient. He had been conscious and lucid on Christmas Eve. I regretted in various ways that we worked so hard to keep him alive. His brother's memories were changed, tainted. He had kept in touch with his family, and he had to report the young man was steadily doing worse. It's not good to pretend you can play God. It's not right.

The morning of the Tet offensive, the telephone rang at 4:30 in the morning. I took the message—the U.S. Embassy had been attacked, we were on red alert, report to the hospital. We were in the hospital by five A.M. at the latest, and we had nothing to do for a period. There were people milling around, it was like a Cecil B. De Mille movie. Smitty, who was the assistant chief nurse, came back and she said, "Go up in the front, we have a war movie up there, only there's no music." So I went up in the front of the hospital in time to see the whole Tiger Regiment, the parachute troopers, marching past the hospital. They had come from back of Tan Son Nhut and then on down this road, and they were on their way to downtown Saigon to fight. They were marching their way along. And over on the left side were these dive bombers coming down and dropping bombs in the rubber plantation area. All you needed was John Wayne somewhere and a great clash of music.

Around eight or nine in the morning, the casualties were coming into the triage area. We started putting names and numbers up in the operating room. And within an hour, we were four hours behind.

Seemed like the VC aimed for joints, wounds of knee, ankle, hand, etcetera. The only Viets we took were abdominal, chest, and head wounds. The American GIs went first to the OR. Sometime around 10 in the morning, my sergeant came to me and said they had a bunch of MPs pinned down in 100 P. Alley. A hundred Piasters was about one dollar, and this was the place where those so inclined could find women for that price. There had been reports that a bunch of officers had been trapped in their quarters nearby, and they sent in two truckloads of MPs to get them out. And of course communication is lost in that kind of situation. In the midst of all the confusion there, the officers had gotten out. They had gotten away, but no one had thought to notify the MPs. I don't know . . . anyhow many things happened in the confusion, and the MPs were sent to evacuate an empty area.

The MPs, like everybody else, were learning to fight a war. And so the officer in charge sent the MPs down 100 P. Alley sitting in trucks. You don't do that. You unload them before you start down the alley, and then you let them go down. You know the war movies are accurate. People dodge from spot to spot. I'm not saying this because I've done it. I'm saying this because the men I've talked to said that there had been a great mistake made in sending them down. Technically, it was proper, but it was not a good choice. Claymore mines had been set off under the deuce-and-a-half trucks they were riding. Don't know whether they were contact or remote control, probably remote. Those who weren't killed by mines were shot by VC in the area. How many there were in the total group that went in, I don't know. I know we had 30–40 bodies brought back to us.

Reinforcements were sent in and they were calling for help to get the men out who were killed, and to help get the men out who were still alive. They needed medics and they needed help in several ways. I sent one man down to help who should have gotten a Silver Star. I have fond memories of that man. I had started out feeling like I should have taken his stripe . . . he had gotten into all kinds of trouble that morning . . . but I couldn't when I found out what he had done. You see, we had already been given orders that because the offensive was about to begin, none of the enlisted personnel were to sleep off post. Everybody was supposed to be in their assigned quarters wherever that might be. This fellow previously had been late a couple of times to work and I had told him to get a new alarm clock. His girlfriend apparently wasn't waking him up in time.

He was an E-7, a sergeant, a 91C. A 91 Charlie has practical-nurse level training, and he had been assigned previously to the 25th Infantry Division in Chu Lai. He was a field medic. He was a good man, no two ways about it; but he had a little problem on his getting back in a hospital situation, that type thing. And that morning, I was in and had talked with the assistant chief nurse, and she talked with the chief nurse about where I'd be working. I left the Renal Unit and went into the triage area to work down there. I asked my sergeant, my NCOIC, if everybody was there. Well no, this one man had not arrived yet. I said, "Well, see if you can get in touch with him or find out what's going on." For his own safety, I wanted him there. I wasn't quite this calm about it, let me put it that way. A little later on about 8 o'clock, 8:15, he still was not there. Finally about 9:30 he came walking down the way. And he and I "discussed" the fact that he was not where he was supposed to have been and that he didn't get in like he was supposed to be in. I probably would have overlooked his—you know—his having slept out if he had arrived on time. Well, we had a discussion. A "moment of prayer," you might say. And you know, I told him I was going to have a stripe. So that was all there was to it. I was going to be sure I did that. He went back up to the unit and then they called sometime later about sending in some medics to help remove the dead MPs.

Anyhow, Mack, my NCOIC, came and told me that—reminded me—that this man had been with the 25th Infantry and had been out in the field; and if anybody was capable of going in there, it was him. He was the only one who had field experience in war. So I said, "Yeah, you can go with him, but keep your fat ass down and don't get hit in it." So he took this particular man and they got some other people, too. And they all went to 100 P. Alley.

Mack came back later on, before they brought the truckloads of bodies in. Mack came back, and he said to me that I could not take this man's stripe, that he had been absolutely magnificent in the things that he had done. He had directed fire. He had moved people. He had helped get people out at considerable risk to himself. From the opinion of Mack, the man should have been awarded a medal. The MPs who were there said that he should have been awarded a medal, and that he should have been put in for the Silver Star. So later on during the day when I saw him, we discussed a few more things and I told him that I would not take his stripe, that I would not ask for it. You can only be an idiot so far, you know, then you stop. And I don't know what happened. Whether the MPs forgot about it, whether somebody else took credit or what, I have no idea. But he was not recommended for a Silver Star. The efforts of that man that day were tremendous. Just tremendous.

We were very, very busy. Nobody really knew what was going on or where people were. When we finally got out of the hospital we saw how close they had come to us. There were bullet holes on a building that was probably, oh maybe, less than a 1,000 feet away from us. You went down to the corner and there were all these chips off the side of the building. When they brought the dead MPs in, the thing was to try to identify the bodies so that the disposition people could have an accurate list of names. It's one of the things that has stayed with me. It is probably one of the sources of my anger with the Vietnam situation. First, I thought there was great stupidity in sending people in trucks down an alley. That was the first and foremost thing, and probably the primary thing all the way around. I was probably irritated, angry that the word didn't get back. In a wartime situation you can't get the word to everybody. There are too many things in war that have balanced on the fact that communication was poor. I think it was looking at the loss of life. Four of us went into the trucks with the bodies stacked up. We then had to move the bodies and go through clothing to check dog tags and for any other form of identification. We found out that night when things had quieted down . . . when the sergeant, lieutenant, and captain of the company came in . . . that we had misidentified two-thirds of the people. They had been sleeping with their dog tags off, when they were supposed to be sleeping with the dog tags on. When they got dressed, when the alert came, they started grabbing dog tags. The ones they grabbed weren't necessarily theirs. They grabbed wallets that weren't necessarily theirs. The bodies had to be reidentified in the operating room we had established as a morgue.

It wasn't a matter of horror. It was like being in a situation totally divorced from the rest of the things that were done that day. People in field units did many things they don't normally do. This was totally foreign to anything I had ever done or had any expectation of doing. There are people in the military who take care of individuals who are dead. That sounds rather gross, but everyone has "a job to do." The bodies had to be brought somewhere, the logical place was the hospital. We had a new operating room without air conditioning, a perfect morgue for a short period of time. Looking at them reminded me of pictures of the Civil War, how they were stacked there. It's a picture in my mind I can bring up. Whether they were all put that way . . . I don't know. None of them were covered, their faces were all looking up at the sky. They were dead. It took me from that point to probably 1977–78 to talk to anybody about it.

People ask me all the time if the war changed me. Well, I don't know if I ever put it all together; except I know that when I finished up my year over there, I wasn't that enthusiastic about the Vietnamese nor about the fact that we were still there. But the politicians run the country. We elect them. If I didn't like what they were doing, I should have voted against them. I may not be totally happy with the things I saw—that occurred; but I was not about to go out and march in a parade. I felt the better way was to change the patterns of people and I was very happy Mr. Johnson decided not to run (for reelection). Either he would have gone down to resounding defeat or we would have become much more involved with Vietnam in some way, because he didn't know how to get us out of it. Johnson's ego was such that he couldn't ever really say no and go backwards, you know, that's the kind of man he was.

When I came home, my mother made the comment to me that I had changed, that things were different. It probably made me short-tempered. I'm probably like a lot of other Vietnam veterans I know, you don't always trust the politicians. That seems to be a syndrome of Vietnam veterans. You don't quite trust the system. I came back from 'Nam into the Burn Unit at BAMC and for four years I still continued to be reminded of Vietnam, because by far the vast majority of our patients were men out of Vietnam. I stayed in the Army, for one thing, because I owed the Army eight years. Well, I could have done a lot of things and gotten myself out. But I stayed because the nurses were excellent, and the corpsmen were very fine people.

I went to Korea as chief nurse, and I did a few other things in the

Army until I retired. I came back to San Antonio, just as I had always done throughout my career. When I first got to know the place in 1960, it was the kind of town you could learn very quickly and drive all over. I used to get off duty at 11:45 or so at night, and another nurse and I would drive over to Zarzamora Street on San Antonio's West Side. We'd go to a drive-in restaurant owned by a man that I had met whose mother . . . let's see, one parent was of German background and the other parent was of Mexican background. We'd get there close to midnight and sit and have supper, stay until maybe 12:30 or one A.M. and then drive to our respective residences and go to bed. And when I came back in '68, I could still drive around San Antonio rather freely, but not as freely as I could before. I tried going over to Zarzamora Street to find that restaurant, and I couldn't find it. The city was not as comfortable. San Antonio had begun to grow and change. There were more things going on.

There were a lot of things that were simpler for the military then, like the kids would come into basic training, go down on Broadway and buy a new car as a second lieutenant with no problems whatsoever. I would say the area was more innocent. I would say the United States, you know, the country generally was more innocent than it is at this point. San Antonio had a comfortable atmosphere. There was no hurry.

I didn't suffer much after the war. A few things bothered me, but nothing major. Personally, I think many nurses probably sublimated their angers into their work, into going to school. If they got out of nursing, they went into something else. I think there might be five percent with PTSD (post-traumatic stress disorder). With me, it's a shortness of temper, an unwillingness to suffer fools. I didn't have that before. Once, here in San Antonio, we had a cleaning lady come in who brought her daughter. The daughter was watching TV while we were eating our dinner. I suddenly realized I couldn't eat while this child had no food. It went back to the times we went to visit this particular orphanage in Vietnam. They'd serve us Cokes and food, and the children would be standing there watching us; and every so often we'd ask ourselves whether these children were getting enough to eat, whether we weren't taking food away from them. I couldn't be sure that this little girl really was watching television.

Jeanne Rivera

I had served in Korea, and I really didn't know whether I wanted to go to Vietnam. I was in Korea when I was 21 and it was kind of a traumatic experience for a 21 year old. Then when Vietnam came around, I was kind of debating whether I wanted to go. I was stationed in Puerto Rico, a pretty good assignment. But somewhere along the line I decided it was my turn to go, so I volunteered by writing a letter saying I'd go to Vietnam. I didn't know it would be so quick. I was called in 15 days. So then I went ahead and took my leave and went over to Vietnam. When I got there, they called me in to . . . let's see I think it was a colonel, I'm not going to mention names . . . but I was called in. They told me that they wanted me to go to Qui Nhon because they were having a problem with the operating room there. The operating room supervisor there wasn't working out. She was very nice . . . I met her. She would probably be a very good supervisor in a hospital that had maybe two operating rooms where she wasn't under a great deal of stress. Vietnam was a stressful situation. You had to be quite strong. The operating room is the center of any activity in a zone like that.

It took me a little while before I could actually start to pick up what was wrong. It took several weeks to analyze what the problem

Jeanne Rivera served as an operating room supervisor in both Qui Nhon and Saigon in 1967–1968. Born in 1928 in Puerto Rico, she retired in 1976 as a lieutenant colonel after 24 years in the Army. She now works as a real estate agent in San Antonio.

was. The problem was that they thought everybody should be there seven days a week, 12 hours a day, whether you were working or not. It didn't make any difference if you had anything to do, you had to stay in that operating room. Right there was an error for the simple reason that in the moments when you don't have anything to do, people should have time off. Because when the casualties start to come in, you have to work around the clock. So people needed to relax away from the operating room. That was one of the problems.

Another problem which was very delicate was that they thought they should have a playroom in the back of the OR area. In other words, they had a room with four beds set up, with radios and record players and everything. And they were walking through the operating room hand in hand, nurses and doctors—officers—with their arms around each other. Here is a situation where you have enlisted people around, and they were angry. Professionalism was gone. Everybody was called by their first names. There wasn't that doctor-nurse or nurse-technician relationship. It had crumbled. And when you have that going on, you don't have an effective working department. So that was my job. I came right out and told them. I said, "First of all I want those beds out of that room over there." And they took me to the commanding officer. Yeah, they took me to the commanding officer and I told him, "Look," I said, "would you like to keep one bed in there?" That was perfectly all right; that could be for the on-call person. In Vietnam, you didn't really need an on-call person, because when the call came everybody got out of bed and had to go over there. But I said, "I'll leave one bed in there." I never knew what went on in that room with the four beds. I don't know, I never saw it . . . I said their personal life is their personal life, I don't really care. But we don't need four beds in a room in the back. What they did there I don't know, but I just didn't want it there. If they wanted to socialize, there were other areas of the compound for that.

When I saw a nurse walking hand in hand with a doctor, I took the nurse aside. I figured that the doctor was the surgical chief's responsibility. So I took the nurse aside and I said to her, "Look, you are a professional woman here. You have enlisted people in this department. I don't want you coming hand in hand with your boyfriend into this operating room anymore." I said, "I don't want any of that to be happening in this operating room. When you leave this department you can do whatever you want. But while you are in this situation, you will definitely not do those things." They had a few names for me, but it didn't matter. I was there to do a job. I didn't care what they thought of me. We got that straightened out.

The operating room itself was in bad condition. It wasn't kept very clean. The paint was chipping off the walls. The enlisted personnel weren't too happy. And I had a very good relationship with my enlisted personnel. That's one of the things that you should always strive for—an extremely good relationship with your enlisted personnel. At the same time, they have to know who's in charge. I had made a choice a long time before I went to Vietnam that it didn't matter to me if they liked me or not, I had to do my job. If they liked me that was fine. But I found out a long time ago that being a Mrs. Nice Guy or Ms. Nice Guy wasn't the way to go. I told my sergeant, "We have to clean this place up, we have to paint it." I said I wanted them to put metal strips up to reinforce the walls. I told them exactly what I wanted them to do. He said, "OK, don't worry about it," because we didn't have any paint, we didn't have any metal. In the next few days I had a pile of metal, I had some paint and everything. I guess he was moonlight requisitioning, you know. We were very busy, but we took time to paint our operating room. We had metal put around the sides. And as a matter of fact, it was one of the showcases in Vietnam. People used to come to look at the operating room.

Then I decided that I wanted to build an intercom system through the operating room so I could pipe in music, if you could believe it. I said to the sergeant, "How can we go about this?" He said, "Don't worry about it." So pretty soon I was seeing all these little boxes in the jeeps . . . tape decks and other sound equipment. A few days later the MPs came around. I was a major by that time. They said, "Major, have you seen any little boxes?" I said, "What are you talking about, Sergeant?" He said, "Well, somebody has stolen all the boxes from our jeeps." I said, "No, I haven't seen a thing."

The CO supported me on everything, because he was a career officer and he wanted the best care possible. His reputation depended on how well this hospital did, because when you start to get casualties your operating room has to perform. If it doesn't perform and it falls way behind and they have to take these casualties to another hospital, that's kind of a detriment. I knew that I was in the driver's seat. There was no doubt about it, and I acted accordingly. Nobody, but nobody, did anything in that operating room—no doctor—nobody did anything in that operating room—no technician—unless it went through me first. Like sometimes, when things slowed, they would try to bring a patient through the door without having scheduled him; and I used to stop them right there at the door and ask them, "Where are you going with that patient? Well, you're not doing anything, I want this patient scheduled before you come in through that door. Nothing is coming in through that door unless you schedule it through me." It was things like that, and that's what you have to be. You don't let up for one moment. I mean these are just "for instances." Once this one doctor came and questioned me about something. He figured there was something that we didn't have enough of, so I said to him, "Look doctor, see over there, that's your sink over there, right? You go scrub your hands there, don't you?" He said, "Yeah?" "And then you go from there and you do the operation?" He said, "Yeah?" "Do I go in there and tell you how to do that operation?" He said, "No." I said, "Well, don't come out here and tell me how to run this operating room!" It was things like that.

The big pushes in the early days were a mess. Things went slowly. For instance, they had been doing things like . . . they said they didn't have enough linen, so they wouldn't drape the patients. They didn't have enough supplies. It was just a disaster. People were working continually, continually, continually, and they were all worn out. It came to my mind, you know, we must be making an awful lot of mistakes when we're working that long under that kind of pressure. I couldn't see the mistakes, but I knew that there had to be mistakes made because of the long, very long hours. You accept that wartime is a situation where you're going to have long hours, but this was ridiculous.

And another thing was that we were running out of things like the linen supply, and the sponges, and the instruments. I was head of CMS, Central Materiel Section, the section that processes all the supplies. So that is one of the first things that you had to do was try to get more people in there to take care of supplies. We had to work long, long hours in order to get the machine moving, ordering more supplies, so we would have a greater amount of supplies and backlog. No one had taken the time to order it, and I don't think that they had an inventory of what it was they needed. Ordering was haphazard. There was no system to consistently replenish the supplies that were used in treating the wounded. For instance, they had these emergency kits that were supposed to have been set up and ready for use. These were the kind that you could attach to the back of jeeps, ready to roll in case of emergency. Well, when I opened them up the emergency equipment was still in the original shipping packages, nothing sterile at all. They come with that packing grease that makes them sort of gooey, but keeps them from rusting. It would have been a disaster if they ever took one of those trucks to a site. I said, "Well, Jeez, when did you last take inventory?" Nobody knew. So I said, "Well, Jeez, we better go take an inventory."

One of the first things I had to do was stagger the schedule. I set it up with four different shifts. They overlapped by an hour. Some people would come at 2:30 in the morning. They would work till 8:30 or whenever things quieted down. I always got people off. And another thing I did that kind of irked people was to say we had to close down one operating room every so often, because these doctors were extremely tired. I mean we're dealing with lives here. These doctors couldn't stay that sharp for this long a period. I had five operating rooms, five or six, something like that in that hospital. So what we did was close one operating room, getting those doctors out of there to rest, even in the worst casualties periods. Consider it. How would you like to be a patient on that table with doctors who were absolutely exhausted? It just can't be. In the long run, we didn't slow anything up. As a matter of fact, we may have done better because people were fresh.

Some of the casualties we got in were just incredible. We had one young man come in who'd been hit by a claymore mine. We had to take both his legs, one arm, half of the other arm. We had to do his head . . . we did neurosurgery, abdominal surgery, and he lived. Now there's one that I prayed, I prayed that he would die. I hated to have to send him home to his mother that way. I used to go over there and visit him in the recovery to see how he was doing. I don't know how many pints of blood we used. Well, those were the kind of cases that we were dealing with constantly. I set up a separate room for minor cases. And what I did with the help of a doctor was—I don't know whether this was right or not—we taught the technicians to do all the minor cases. Things like shrapnel under the skin . . . you open the skin up, take it out. And they did very well. We utilized everything and everybody. Most of the doctors, nurses, and technicians were devoted to their duty, really living up to the motto "duty, honor, country."

But not everyone was always so helpful. I happened to be in the triage area one day when it wasn't very busy. They were just treating one of the GIs for something minor. So I was there and I heard this noise. I started to look around and I noticed that there were two Vietnamese on stretchers on the ground, covered with mud. I said, "What's wrong with these people?" The nurse turned around and said, "Oh, these GIs brought them in here. They were buried alive." And I said, "What are you doing for them?" They said, "Nothing, they're going to die." I said, "You mean you're not going to even touch them?" And the doctors were there and they said, "No, we're not going to do anything." Well, I tell you, that's the worst experience I've had in my life. I mean this was the mentality we had over there. This was the difference between Vietnam and Korea, right there. I got so upset and I started to lose my temper with this nurse. She happened to be a captain. And they called the chief nurse, who came and asked, "What's going on here?" I said, "I'll tell you what's going on," I said, "They don't want to do anything for this husband and wife over here and they don't have anything to do!" So this nurse said, "Well, they're going to die . . ." blah, blah, blah. And the chief nurse said, "Jeanne, if you want to do something for them that's fine with me." So I went over and these two GIs, two technicians, came with me. And oh, they said, "Boy are we glad you came in . . . we want to do something for these people." And then that nurse came over and she said to me, "Well, if you want to do something take them outside and wash them off outside." Can you imagine? There was no reason for it whatsoever.

That's how they treated the Vietnamese. I mean it was just a warped mentality. I looked at this nurse, I just couldn't believe it. So the technicians brought over the suction tubes. Of course I don't know how long they had been sitting there. And as soon as I put the suction tube in and started to take the mud out of their nose and everything like that, they passed away, one right after the other. I guess they were really dying, but they hadn't tried to do anything for them. I always considered myself a coward for not having taken that further, because I really believe that that nurse should have been court martialed and those doctors the same thing. I mean, to this day that's one of the worst experiences I have ever had in my life. And yet, this young woman who was there professed to be a very religious individual. She was a Catholic. I happen to be a Catholic myself, and she used to walk around with the sisters and the priest all the time. To this day, if I could ever find her . . . I don't even remember her name. I think I blanked it out of my head but that was one of the things that I regretted not having gone further on. You know, you don't want to rock the boat. I hadn't been there very long when this happened. To this day, that's something that really, really, really bothers me. I thought it was one of the most inhumane things I had ever seen. I never felt that anyone should come before anyone else. I always felt that a human being is a human being, whether they be Vietnamese or American. It never, never bothered me that way. As far as I was concerned, it was whoever was the sickest would go first. We didn't have that many Vietnamese come in, so I never really had to choose. But that was definitely one of the worst things that I saw there.

We all saw a lot of things we didn't like for one reason or another. I wasn't too thrilled over how the intelligence people used to handle the Vietnamese who came in. I mean it was pretty bad. We'd get calls that they were bringing Vietnamese in, and when the helicopter got there it would be empty. If they got to the hospital alive, it didn't matter how sick or bad off they were. They would take them by the hair, pull their head back, and ask them questions and things like that, right in the hospital. I just turned my back on it. This is how it was. I mean, unfortunately, you have . . . it's a terrible feeling that you get inside of you. In Korea I never saw as much brutality as I saw in Vietnam. In Korea it was like a naive people at war. In Vietnam, it was just like there was no morality. It was hard for me to understand some of the mentality there.

After I'd been there for six months I figured that the place was pretty well settled down, and I was ready for another assignment. So I asked to go to Saigon. And it so happened that they were having the same problems in Saigon. So I was shipped off—I went off to

Saigon. The hospital there was the 3rd Field. I was getting bored in Qui Nhon because everything was finally running along pretty smoothly. And when I got to Saigon it was funny . . . I was there for a few days, and the chief nurse called me in and she said, "Boy, I thought I was going to get another nurse that nobody wanted." They had sent my papers in recommending me for the bronze star, and she said, "I'm glad that we are really getting someone good."

In Saigon we had an operating room, but they wanted to build a new one. The idea was to keep the old one going and build a new one at the same time. That was my assignment. They had all this new equipment and this hospital was to be the showcase of Vietnam. Everything was closer together. Triage was right in front of the operating room. Right behind was the CMS. So I had control of both areas, plus I spent a lot of time in triage. We got a lot more casualties there than in Qui Nhon. There were big pushes near Saigon constantly. As a matter of fact, the shots would come into the triage area in Saigon where in Qui Nhon we were pretty far away from where the actual action was.

As soon as we knew there was a push coming I would start telling everybody to get the operating room ready. Usually we had one big instrument table towards the back. And we would go take all the instruments from there to set up the tables for heavy volume, some-times two operating room tables in one room. And then we'd have that back table, which we used for instruments. We'd come in and keep replacing the instruments on the back tables throughout sur-gery. Now that's not the best technique in the world, because they say you shouldn't keep open instruments when you're going to use them on other patients. They were always sterile, of course. I thought it worked pretty well because our infection rate in Vietnam was very low considering the type of casualties we used to get there. I'd have the CMS group in there so they could start processing packs. Then I'd go out into the triage area with a doctor and we used to look and see what kind of patients we were getting in. We were getting them ready to go into the operating room. Some of them we didn't even undress in the triage area. We just took them the way they were right into the operating room, because they were the more severely wounded.

The wounds were always the dirtiest ones imaginable. Punji sticks, mud in the wounds, the material of their fatigues into the wounds, compound fractures, I mean big, big, big wounds. The compound fractures came from shrapnel and bullets hitting bones. We had bleeding iliacs. Those are the arteries that feed the legs. I remember once that I had to put my whole hand with a sponge in there trying to hold it so this particular fellow wouldn't bleed to death. By the time we got him to the operating room, I'd had my hand in there for awhile already. They cleaned around it, and got their instruments ready so they could go in there with a Kelly or some other instrument and tie off the iliac for awhile until they could see what was going on. After cleaning it, they'd try to get it back together or put some kind of a little piece of prosthetic material in there to tie the two ends together. In that particular case we saved his leg, and saved him.

The nurse never scrubbed in any of the cases. My nurses were the supervisors of each one of those rooms. One nurse was usually between two rooms or one nurse in each room depending on how much personnel we had. The technicians did all the scrubbing. In the meantime, what I was doing was coordinating between the recovery room, the operating room, CMS, and the triage area. I was the runner for everything. I ran if they needed blood. If they needed more supplies I ran and got the supplies. I was the one who cleaned the instruments, put them out, got them ready. I did hire a Vietnamese woman and I trained her to clean the instruments, because I didn't think that we needed technicians, or nurses, or anybody who could serve in the rooms to do this type of work. There wasn't anything I didn't do. When I went to Vietnam I weighed 110 pounds. When I came out of Vietnam I weighed 87 pounds. I couldn't eat. I got to the point in Saigon where I could not eat anymore. I was on milk. All I could drink was that reconstituted milk. The CO once asked me how I did it. I don't know how I did it.

The laundry, believe it or not, was a critical link in this whole coordinating effort between doctors, supplies, and the rest. Once I had a run-in with the laundry . . . we were having a big push and I went to the supply room and the major was there, and I said, "How come I'm not getting any linen out of here?" He said, "Well, my people have to rest." I said, "Your people don't have to have rest." I said, "As long as there is a push on, and the OR is going, your job is to supply me." He said, "Oh no we're not." I said, "Oh yes you are." He said, "No, I run this department." I said, "Well you wait right there." And I went and got the CO and he came over and he said, "You get those laundry machines moving!" They had these big industrial-size washing machines. We didn't have a problem from then on, as long as I was there at least.

Sometimes we were seven–eight hours behind with casualties. The way I figured it was seven or eight hours behind. At some point, I'd close down one operating room at a time, and I'd tell the people to go rest. I'd have food brought right into a room in the back. So while somebody else was cleaning the OR, they'd go in there and they would eat. I never had anybody go hungry in an operating room. I never felt any conflict about closing an OR. I felt I was doing everyone concerned a favor. Sometimes I'd get into trouble. I mean I'd have to get into arguments over these things. But I felt that I was doing those people, those GIs who were coming in, a favor. I was thinking of them more than maybe some other person who was just interested in numbers. I think that everybody, the doctors, the CO, and everyone respected me for it, and I think my people respected me because I was thinking of them. I didn't want any of them to collapse on me. I mean we had a young, very young, hospital crew, and we worked just day after day. We got to a point where there was so much blood, there was so much that I had holes put in the bottom of the operating room so we could clean the floor. We used tons and tons of saline to clean off these wounds that we had. But when I was there, the patients were always completely draped for every surgical operation. That's the linen you put over a patient to make the area surgically clean. You put them on so that only the area you're going to operate in is exposed. This way, you don't get this unsterile area exposed. You don't run the risk of getting dirt or other things, bacteria, into the wound.

The chief of surgery was the one with the most experience. He did the triage. I found that we never had to make too many choices. The only cases that I found where we had to make those choices were the head wounds, because we had to wait for awhile to see how it went. For instance, a lot of them got drugs prior to arriving. So if their pupils were dilated, it might be because they've gotten some kind of drug. This was the only case that we usually had to put aside and wait to see how their symptoms developed. I don't think we ever had to make a conscious decision as to "he's going to wait" or "he's not going to wait." That one fellow I was talking about, the one who lost all those limbs and his eyes . . . we should have put him aside probably, but he wouldn't have made it because he was so terribly wounded. But we took him first, before everyone else. And that's probably what saved his life, fortunately or unfortunately. I felt that probably if we had left that young boy behind that we wouldn't have had to send him to his parents like that. If we would have waited he would have probably died. This fellow didn't even have eyes. We had to take his eyes because they had popped out. He looked like one of those scary masks that you put on where the eyes fall forward. That's what he looked like. And you say to yourself, "God, what am I doing sending this boy home?" All I could think of was his mother. Not his father. I thought of his mother. His mother had this child, and now she's going to get him back just like a child again. What is she going to embrace? He was just a trunk. Now, that's the feeling that I got. But I never felt that I played God. I just thought that it was a matter of—in that particular case, you know— that if we had waited. . . .

This one doctor said to me, "Now, Jeanne, don't get all upset about that because we're here to save lives. That's our purpose—to save lives." That was the truth. It's not our decision who lives and who dies. That's what we came to feel. So after that things didn't bother me. Well, they bothered me, but at the same time I said it's not. . . . If God wants this young man to live, there's a purpose for it. It wasn't fatalism. I don't believe in fatalism. But I believe there are certain laws of nature. I'm a very religious person. And I believe that if God sees fit to take you, he'll take you. If God doesn't, then you're going to live. Today people say, "Well, they're going to turn this machine off on this individual," and they say the doctor tries to play God. "If we turn this machine off, this person is going to die." And they turned the machine off on Karen Ann Quinlan, but she lived for many years. So it's not in our hands.

I never believed I was playing God. I believed that I was doing what I was educated to do. And I believe that Vietnam for many of us . . . like they say you have your moment of greatness, and it comes and goes and you don't even know it happened. Well, that was what happened to me. That was one of my moments of greatness. I couldn't believe that I could work such long hours and keep my brain so sharp. I saw it all around me with the men and women I worked with. There was such a feeling of togetherness on the job as we accomplished our mission. And I felt that the stricter I was and the more efficient the unit became, the stronger the feelings were that grew between the people. You were working like a smooth machine.

I remember that I went out to the triage area and there was this one fellow who was wounded badly. He must have been an MP, because he had this guard dog still leashed to his arm. And we couldn't get to him because they had brought him in with this guard dog. Nobody wanted to get close to him, because they were afraid the dog would bite. I can't remember exactly what had happened to the guy, but I know he was wounded very severely. He had no control over his dog anymore. But they had brought him in on one of those flat beds. They used to come right into the area with the wounded on the top of them. And these GIs had just picked him and his dog up and plopped him down in the triage area. But they finally sent for the MPs, and the MPs came and took the dog. I don't remember what happened to the guy after that.

Once they were having a hard time getting this young boy to sleep. So I went in there and I looked at him, and he said, "Oh please, please they're going to take my legs. I know they're going to take my legs." And I said "Yeah, they're going to take your legs." He asked, "Have you ever seen people like this before?" Of course that's where my experience from Korea came in. I had been involved in rehabilitation. So I said, "Yeah, I've seen lots of guys like you." He asked, "How do they do after?" I said, "When you get your prosthetic devices you're going to walk just as proud as any man there is." He looked at me and he said, "Oh, thank you nurse." And then he let them put him to sleep. Just accidentally I walked into the room. Nobody sent for me. I just accidentally walked into that room. It was little situations like that where I think sometimes a woman's touch really came to the aid of a lot of these severely wounded GIs. Sometimes all they needed was just someone to talk to them. I think talking to them . . . sometimes they thought I was their mother. "Mom," you know, calling me "Mom." They were so out of it.

I remember one fellow didn't even know that when I took his boot off, I took his foot. I was in the triage area and this one fellow was sitting there, and I knew that he had to go into surgery because I saw the blood on his leg. So I just went ahead and pulled my scissors and started cutting through his fatigues. I started yanking his boot off, and when I finally got it—his foot was in it. But he was out of it. I mean, I could just tell that the medics had either drugged him a lot, or he had been on something himself. It's just that he was in real bad shape.

We had to handle the crash of two helicopters that were going to the Bob Hope show. They collided in midair and they brought these GIs to the hospital. You could have picked them up like they were a suit of clothes on a hangar, and they would have dropped down limp because their bones were broken in so many places. Choppers came straight down. They looked perfect. No blood, no nothing. The impact of the crash had broken and ruptured everything. They were all dead. The rudders had flown off, their brains had herniated. And physically, sometimes, they even looked all right. But I think that their respiration was completely cut off by the herniation of the brain.

Because of the medications our corpsmen gave our soldiers, the triage area was usually very quiet as far as screaming and crying goes. You could tell the difference when the Vietnamese came in, because they weren't medicated or anything. And that's when you see this terrible agony of pain. And I think that's why you're not that affected by all that's going on when you are in that situation—usually it's so quiet. And you couldn't feel their pain that much. So you could maintain yourself and control yourself a lot better. When I have to deal with people who are in a lot of pain, it's just like I've got to force myself, I mean, really force myself to do it. It's just breaking me up inside when I have to hurt them so bad. Like in burn cases. But with the GIs—like when I pulled that guy's shoe off, he didn't complain. He didn't even know his foot was in his shoe. That's a lot easier than walking into this madhouse of people screaming in pain. I don't think you could take it.

I think that sometimes war breeds cruelty. I knew this one officer who patrolled with what you might call "hit squads." They used to stay up in the mountains and sit all night with these high-powered rifles with infra-red telescopes, popping people off. I mean, he didn't know whether they were Viet Cong or what they were. I'm sure that happened during World War II and Korea. In Korea, at least, I never heard of anything like that. But in Vietnam it was the thing to do. There was no denying it. And I think that probably happens in all the wars. I don't think that there was any difference between them, because my brother told me about World War II. He was in the Philippines, and he said that they used to give them prizes for how many teeth they would bring in that had gold fillings from the dead Japanese. In Vietnam it was commonplace. It was just like that was the norm.

If you were a GI, it was like you were working out there as an individual and you just had the support of maybe your one buddy. But you didn't have the support of the officers and you didn't have the support from Washington maybe. They lied to you a lot. And if you came into Saigon . . . I saw how the GI came in, muddy and everything. They saw how some of the officers lived in those air-conditioned trailers, nice clubs, and all that stuff. I mean, you just wonder what they must have thought. In Korea we all lived the same. We didn't take a bath every day, we didn't have all the niceties. But in Vietnam, the officers and some of the enlisted people lived very, very nicely. There was no meat in the mess hall sometimes, but the officers had shrimp and lobster and steaks at the parties. Any party you went to, they had steaks there, yet in the mess hall there wasn't any of that.

I was extremely young and naive in Korea. The war was not as horrible, but in some ways it made a bigger impression on me. The casualties were not as severe as what you saw in Vietnam. Korea was different. In Korea there was a front line. By the time I got patients, they had been through a MASH unit. The chain of evacuation didn't matter as much in Vietnam. The wounded went to the nearest place because, really, there was no front line. During Korea, the Army was like a family. When you were assigned to a post in the states or anywhere, you got a good greeting from everybody. Everything was done within the post. The officers club was always crowded. Everybody was a family. You went overseas as groups,

Lt. Jacqueline Navarra with an injured orphan (upper left) and meeting a wounded G.I. (upper right), Quang Tri. *Courtesy Jacqueline N. Rhoads*

Jacqueline Navarra Rhoads, 1986. *Courtesy Jacqueline N. Rhoads*

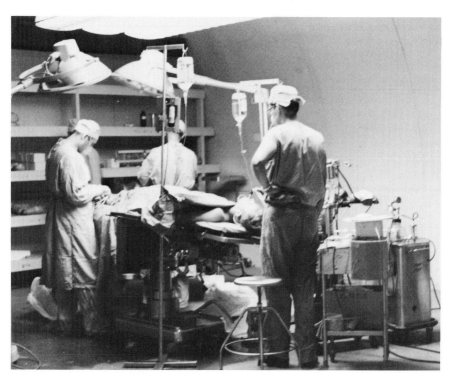

Operating room at the 18th Surgical Hospital, Quang Tri, 1971. *Courtesy Jacqueline N. Rhoads*

67th Evacuation Hospital, Qui Nhon. *Courtesy Deanna McGookin*

Captain Lorraine Boudreau with Vietnamese child, Chu Lai, 1969.
Courtesy Lorraine Boudreau

Lorraine Boudreau, 1986.
Courtesy Dan Freedman

Medics unloading a helicopter with incoming wounded, Quang Tri. *Courtesy Jacqueline N. Rhoads*

A bunker at the 18th Surgical Hospital, Quang Tri. *Courtesy Jacqueline N. Rhoads*

Medcaps, Qui Nhon. *Courtesy Deanna McGookin*

Montagnard mother and child. Her severely wounded husband received treatment at the 67th Evacuation Hospital in Qui Nhon. *Courtesy Deanna McGookin*

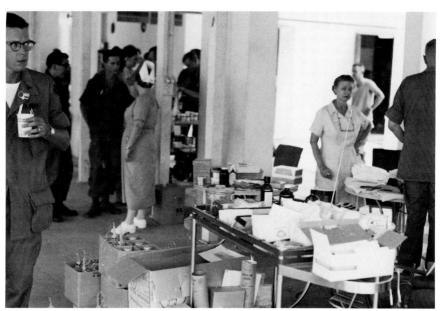

Major Lois Johns and Red Cross worker in triage area on the first day of the Tet Offensive, Saigon, 1968. *Courtesy Lois Johns*

Major Anna Smith ("Smitty") and Major Lois Johns, Saigon, 1968. *Courtesy Lois Johns*

Lois Johns, 1986. *Courtesy Dan Freedman*

Major Jeanne Rivera, Saigon, 1968. *Courtesy Jeanne Rivera*

Jeanne Rivera, 1986.
Courtesy Dan Freedman

Actor Hugh O'Brian visits Bien Hoa, December 1965. (Left to right) Lt. Dawn Krueger, Hugh O'Brian, Lt. Lorraine Boudreau, Lt. Carol Burke. *Courtesy Lorraine Boudreau*

Lt. Jacqueline Navarra in helicopter flight gear, Quang Tri. *Courtesy Jacqueline N. Rhoads*

Unidentified nurse learning how to load, shoot and disarm a machine gun. *Courtesy Jacqueline N. Rhoads*

Lt. Karen Bush, Pleiku, 1967. *Courtesy Karen Bush*

Karen Bush, 1986. *Courtesy Dan Freedman*

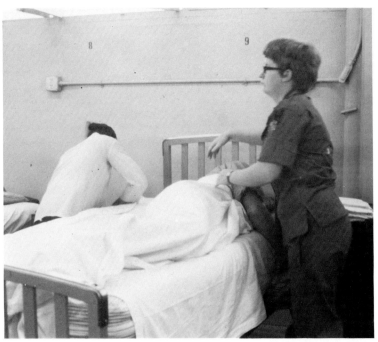

Lt. Deanna McGookin with a patient at the 67th Evacuation Hospital, Qui Nhon, 1968. *Courtesy Deanna McGookin*

Lt. Colonel Deanna McGookin, 1986. *Courtesy Deanna McGookin*

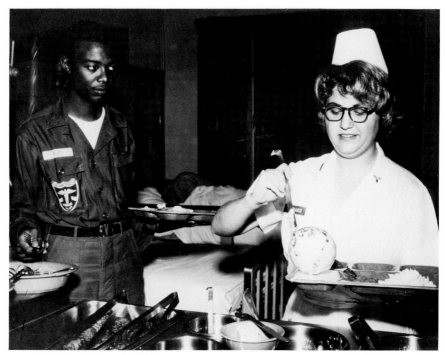

Lt. Shirley Menard serves breakfast to patients on her ward at the 8th Field Hospital, Nha Trang, 1966. *Courtesy Department of the Army*

Shirley Menard, 1986.
Courtesy Dan Freedman

Lt. Joan Waradzyn posing for a picture taken by one of her patients at the 18th Surgical Hospital, Cam Ranh Bay, 1969. *Courtesy Joan Thomas*

Joan Waradzyn Thomas, 1986. *Courtesy Dan Freedman*

hospitals went over as groups. If you went there, you felt like you were a part of a family. Vietnam came at a time when that didn't exist anymore. People lived off post. During Korea, everybody lived on post. It didn't matter who you were. You couldn't live off post. Everybody lived there so everybody knew each other. The Army's not that way anymore. You might hardly know anybody that you worked with. You just know them the eight or so hours you're there, just like any other job. And from there you go home. In Vietnam, that's the kind of individual you were getting. You were getting people who were very independent, who hadn't had this feeling of togetherness when they came, and it was just completely different. It's like they were eons apart.

I was a very patriotic person. I thought that whatever we were doing, we were doing because it was right. In the beginning, I didn't want to go to Vietnam because I had been to Korea. And I knew about the terrible hours you get to keep and the terrible trauma you were always facing. I didn't know if I wanted to see that again. But I said to myself, "Well, it's my patriotic duty. I'm in the Army. Our goal is to conserve our fighting strength and that's where I belong." You're in the Army because eventually there's going to be a war. Let's face it, that's what you're there for. It's not to have it easy. It's to be where you're needed the most in time of conflict. So that's why I went to Vietnam. It was my duty to go there. But when I got back from Vietnam, I was no longer the red, white, and blue person I used to be. My ideas had changed on that. I found I used to believe everything the government told me. I thought I was going over there because I had—I had read a lot on the "domino theory." You know, that if Vietnam falls, all of Southeast Asia would fall. And I believed that these people were being invaded by an enemy that they didn't want. And I believed we were supporting the right government in Vietnam. And then, once I went there, I saw what a catastrophe the government was, and that the government was really lying to the people in the United States. I mean, our people were lying to us and lying to everybody. And then when I found out that we were getting out of Vietnam, and all those people had died—died for nothing. And all those legs and everything that were left over there. And all those poor guys who are here that nobody cares about, crippled and lying over here in the VA hospitals. I don't believe half, not even half of what the government tells me now. I don't believe anything as a matter of fact. I used to think that we never did anything wrong. I was that naive. I really thought that the government would never be oppressive to any other government. I thought that we were above-board in all of our dealings until I went to Vietnam and came back. I question everything now. And of course, most of all, I question getting involved in war unless we go there to win, and unless there is a really clear-cut reason for being there. Otherwise forget it.

Occasionally, something will trigger me off a little bit, and I get very teary-eyed. I get extremely teary-eyed at anything that reminds me of some of the things that happened over there. I sometimes think of it, and it's just like a flash. I'll think of it and I say, "My God, why did I send him home to his mother?" I still kind of blame myself for that. Sometimes I'll sit there and think of it. Sometimes I'm in bed and some of these things come back to me and I blame myself, like for instance, what happened with the two Vietnamese. That comes back to me a lot. I feel that I neglected my duty for not having reported that nurse to a higher authority. Because I really believe to this day that she doesn't belong in nursing.

As a whole, I thought it was a wonderful experience for me and I don't regret having been over there. And if I were called again to go somewhere else, I would go again, even at the age I am now. I still have orders where if they wanted to call me back, they could. It was a wonderful, horrible experience. I felt that everything that I had ever learned in my career, I put to use in Vietnam. I felt that I was in control. I wasn't a subservient individual, and that's how nurses are generally perceived. Vietnam gave me a feeling of accomplishment. I actually had the power to do what I wanted to do. In the states, you don't have that. You have to go through a million people before you can get anything done. Where I was, if I wanted something done, I did it. It seemed that people didn't question what I wanted to do. And that was because of the need, the urgency. The operating room is the single most important place in a hospital in that sort of mission.

As a manager I made . . . I don't know if you would call it a mistake, but I feel responsible. When I was in Qui Nhon, this one hospital further north was real, real busy. So they said they wanted to borrow some of our personnel, because we were doing so well, I guess. They needed operating room nurses and anesthetics people. So I told the chief nurse, "What you should do is send me up there, because I think what they have up there is mismanagement. They don't need these extra people." I said, "Why don't you just send me?" So she said, "Nope, nope. We're not going to send you. You pick whoever you want to send." So I did. I picked one male nurse, an anesthetist, and I picked two of my female nurses. And they used to call me, saying, "Major, can't you get us back over there? We're not doing anything over here." They never got back. They crashed into the mountain on their way home to Qui Nhon. They never came back. We never found out if it was shot down or if it was mechanical failure. They crashed into a mountain. And one of them—the young male nurse—his wife hadn't even delivered their baby yet. And he was gone. One of the nurses had come over from Poland. Her family were refugees. I found this out after. She had come over from Poland and they were refugees and she was so proud of being a nurse and being in the service. And of course, I remember writing a letter to her mother, and that really hurt. I picked them. I mean, yeah, I know somebody had to do it, but it doesn't change how I perceive it. To this day I say, "My God, that could have been, probably could have been me instead of them." And I had to sit down and write her mother a letter which was really, really. . . . Yet when I wrote it then, it didn't feel as bad as when I think of it now. And I remember we collected money to start a scholarship fund in her name. I cannot remember her name. One of these days I'm going to Washington and I'm going to look up their names.

People would complain to me about the way certain things got done, little procedures we had. I used to ask them, the doctors mostly, "Is this operating room functioning to your satisfaction?" And they would say, "Oh yeah, sure." I'd say, "Then you shouldn't question what I do. I mean, the job is getting done, it's running better than before." And he'd say, "Oh yeah, sure." There was one little incident when I was in Qui Nhon. I was so tired. We'd worked a long stretch and, although people were getting off, I was still there. And the casualties were still coming in, but I was so tired that I just couldn't go on. I took the nurse who was second to me and I said to her, "Look, I have this all outlined here. Everything, how it's going to be done." I used to make long sheets of paper of how everything was going to be done. I said, "I want you to take over for a little while. I'm going to go to bed. I have to get some rest." So I took off. I don't know how long it was, but it wasn't very long when the chief nurse came and woke me up. She said "Colonel so-and-so wants you back. What are you doing? Are you"—what was the word she used, I can't remember—"are you deserting him?" I said, "Am I deserting him?" I said, "I need rest." She said, "He wants you back." I mean I'm humble, but I know the feeling was that if I wasn't there then everything was going to go wrong. This doctor-colonel needed me. I was his; I mean, if I wasn't there, that place was going to fall apart. And I had to get up, put my clothes on and go over there. And I went up to him and I told him "This operating room, has this been functioning, or what?" And he said, "Yes." I said, "Then you have to let me make my decisions. I knew that this hospital could work for a few hours, this operating room could work for a few hours, and I needed to rest." And he said, "Oh, I'm sorry" and he kind of apologized to me. I knew the place wouldn't fall apart without me. But that's the way he felt.

A lot of the nurses over there were much younger than I was. They were 21. When I went to Vietnam I was in my 30s. So they were the ones who needed the experience. They were the ones you had to hold together, not only professionally, but a lot of them had mental problems that you had to solve. There were broken love affairs—that was the least that I needed. But I had several nurses who had problems with that. They were young women. They were promised the world. The men rotated, and I had these hysterical young women on my hands. The typical thing was that you had this male officer who's married, say, and he'd tell this nurse, "Well I'm separated from my wife." When they first came in country, I used to take them aside and say, "Look I'm going to sit you down and I'm going to tell you this, that a lot of these doctors and a lot of these officers or enlisted people are going to tell you that they're separated from their wives or that they're not married. I want you to come and talk to me about it before you establish any relationship with them, because you are going to get yourself into deep trouble." I said, "They'll tell you that they're separated from their wives. That's because they're here!" They all thought I was an old fuddy-duddy. There were a

certain number of them who contemplated suicide. I had one close
call, but she was not successful. She was pretty bad when she left
us. They shipped her off to Japan.

I was born in a very small town in Puerto Rico, Vega Alta. My
people were very prominent in politics, my mother's side especially.
As a matter of fact, my mother's father was a mayor and a brother
had been treasurer of Puerto Rico. We were all lawyers and teachers
and professional people. My father was a pharmacologist. He ran a
drug store. He did a lot of things because it was during the Depression years. He did whatever he could to keep us alive. We went back
and forth from Puerto Rico and the United States. And finally, I
came to the United States in my sophomore year in high school and
went to Julia Richman High School in New York City. It was an all-
girl school then. We lived in Manhattan on Riverside Drive, around
109th Street, not too far from Columbia University. And then we
moved to New Jersey, to Riverside, which is near Camden. All my
life—I don't know why—I thought I was going to be a nurse.

I probably would have thought of being a doctor. But in those
days there just wasn't an opportunity for a woman to become a doctor. Maybe some of them did, but I never knew or saw any. So I was
going to become a nurse. I went to a Catholic hospital in Trenton,
New Jersey, a three-year school. St. Frances Hospital School of
Nursing in Trenton. And I think that is where I got my best training
for the Army. The Sisters had a chain of command just like the
military. I remember we worked 12 hours a day, six days a week.
There was nothing but 12-hour shifts in these Catholic hospitals.
Everything had to be clean, just like the Army. The Sisters would
come and inspect. They'd send us into an area to clean and everything had to be tip-top. And if the Sister went in there and found one
corner on one bed was wrong, she made us strip the whole place
down and start all over again. I remember when they knew I was
going to go into the service, they said, "Miss Rivera, you're not
going to make it. You don't know how strict they are in the Army."
So when I got into the Army, I said, "Oh, my God this is easy." The
Army was easy compared to having been with those Sisters. They
taught me discipline. Things had to be done at a certain time, you
reported in at a certain time. You worked whether you were sick or

not. I remember one time I had a temperature of 102 degrees, and
they said to me, "What's the best thing for it, Miss Rivera?" And I
asked, "What, Sister?" "Work. You have to work it all out of you."

I can be honest about why I went into the military. I thought that it
would be an attention getter, the uniform. And I needed that support, coming from a minority group. I don't know why, because in
those days there wasn't that anti-Puerto Rican feeling in New York
that there is today, because there were very few Puerto Ricans. So it
wasn't that. But it was a step ahead. Stepping up into a uniform
meant that I was somebody. I never thought of discrimination when I
was a civilian. I didn't feel it until I came into the service. There just
wasn't a problem in New York. Our English was always good because we had tutors in Puerto Rico who taught us. I didn't speak with
an accent, except maybe a New York accent.

I came into the Army in 1952. Most of the other nurses were from
the East around Philadelphia. They were Catholics. They were Irish.
A lot of Irish. It wasn't until I came back from Korea that I felt real
prejudice. Two times I felt that way in the Army. Once was when I
came back from Korea and I was teetering on the idea of whether I
was going to get out or not. The second time was when I had to work
under this chief nurse. I got out. She definitely made my life miserable, absolutely miserable. She looked for every opportunity there
was to make my life miserable. So I got out of the service for three
years and then I came back in. In between that time I went into
public health, and I worked with the migrant farm workers out there
in New Jersey. That was very interesting. You talk about people who
had been discriminated against . . . they're the ones. And then my
father died. So unfortunately, he didn't leave too much. I took on the
responsibility of my mother. Although I had a brother and two sisters, I'm in the middle and there always seems to be one in the
family who takes on the burden. So I said, "Well, I can't make it. I
definitely cannot make it in civilian practice. I cannot make enough
money to support my mother. And I have to think of medical care
for both of us." I decided the Army was the place. I could claim my
mother as my dependent, so that's what I did.

I rejoined the service. I came back in 1957. That's when I made
another conscious decision—that I didn't want to work all those
night shifts. And for a selfish reason, I went into the operating room

and became an operating room nurse. Because I figured I could take
call a lot better than I could take working all those night shifts. I
could never sleep during the day. I'm not that kind of person. I'm a
day person. I can do a lot of things during the day, but come six in
the evening, forget me. I'm out of it. Some people work better at
night, but I'm definitely a day person.

I made a conscious decision that I wasn't going to get married
because I didn't want to have children. I'm self-centered enough that
I knew I didn't want to get involved with anybody. My father did
everything. He made all the decisions. But my mother was also a
very, very, very strong woman and there was conflict. He was strong
and she was strong. And we had these terrible conflicts within the
family. My mother probably should never have been a housewife.
She should have gone into a career, but in those days there was no
way for a woman to do that kind of thing, at least not in our circle.
And I look at that, that kind of mindset. I didn't think that I could
have anybody telling me what to do. Of course, I chose the Army,
which may seem contradictory. It always upsets me that nurses don't
take a more active part in the decision-making of a hospital, and in
the care of the patient. I have lived with that all my life . . . situations where I had no power. Vietnam was just about the only excep-
tion. I don't know why I ever stayed in the Army as long as I did. I
like to have power. And in nursing you don't have it.

In Vietnam or elsewhere, if the nurses weren't there, the hospital—as far as I'm concerned—would collapse. See, that's a conflict
that I've had all my life; and if I had come of age in today's world I
probably would not have been a nurse. I know that I could have been
a wonderful business woman. I'm very outspoken. You know, one
nurse once told me I'm not a diplomat. "You have to be diplomatic."
And I said, "Well, why do I have to be diplomatic?" I said, "I'm
going to tell you what I feel." I'm quiet, I don't chit-chat. I cannot sit
there and chit-chat. It makes me very nervous . . . when these
chiefs came from Washington, I'd sit there in these meetings and
they'd sit there and spout off on this theoretical level, everything
from a textbook. And I knew that in the field they weren't doing it
that way. But these people were the experts. Those things really
irked me. I don't have a master's degree. I have my bachelor's degree,
but I don't have a master's. They think that sometimes just because

you have that education, that it makes you a good educator. Or it makes you a good administrator. It doesn't. I think that's something that you have to work at. You're not born an administrator. You have to work at it. And you have to take into account not just getting the job done, although that's important, but also your personnel—what their strengths and weaknesses are, how you're going to approach them.

Before I went to Vietnam I was at Fort Sam Houston, and that's where I had this chief nurse who tried to destroy me. I was a captain. She'd sit there and she'd start talking about Mexicans this and Mexicans that. I'm not Mexican, but I have the name Rivera. I was her second in rank. She was a colonel, a big disparity there. I was the second and she was trying to put this other junior captain in charge over me. I finally had to go to her and tell her, you know, I said, "Look, I'm your second in command here and I. . . ." That's when I first made my conscious decision that I wasn't going to take it anymore. I remember that very clearly, that was when I said "I am not." If this ruins my career so be it. I am not going to take this crap from anybody else anymore. I said to myself, "I am intelligent and I can work and I can do the job." And that's exactly what I told her. So she sent me over to Beach Pavilion, which was the worst. And left me there to sink or swim. I used to have to get up at four in the morning to get there at five. Everything I did was wrong. I used to hear her with the doctors, "Well, you can thank Captain Rivera for that." Finally, the chief nurse came to me once and she says, "I'm going to take you out of there because you're going to be ruined." She told me, "You've already got one bad efficiency;" and I said, "No, I'm going to stick it out. I'm going to stick it out." So she sends me back and it got worse. Finally she says, "I'm taking you out and sending you over to Institute of Surgical Research," which is the burn unit. She tried everything she could think of. Situations like that, I guess I was kind of naive. I should have taken her to the IG (Inspector General). But I didn't.

That chief nurse helped me to decide that I was not going to play "nice person" anymore. Because I was the only Puerto Rican, I felt that they were trying to make me feel inferior. I felt that. I felt that from a lot of people there. I finally sat myself down and I said "Now wait a minute. Why take this kind of crap from these people?" And I made that decision there. But I felt the same kind of thing all through my career. I know that I was discriminated against when I wanted to go into recruiting and they wouldn't send me, even though I was recommended for it. I'm almost sure they didn't take me because I was Puerto Rican. I'm positive of it. So I felt the discrimination. But that didn't deter me from my goal. I always had to be proving myself. Because of that, rather than in spite of it, I became what I was.

The time finally came when I had to get out. I thought that civilian nursing would be worse than the Army. Civilian nurses have even less authority. They have even less to say than in the Army. I may be wrong about that, since I haven't worked in a civilian hospital in a long time. In any case, civilian nursing wasn't something I considered for myself after the Army, because I just knew that I was through with nursing, that I wanted to go into something where maybe I'd have a little bit more control over my life. After leaving the Army, I didn't do anything for a couple of years, and then I went into real estate. I feel I can do whatever I want now. All through the Army I was remodeling—remodeling operating rooms. Well, now I'm remodeling houses. I bought an old farm house and redid it, and now I'm buying another one and I'm going to redo it, too. Once I remodel them, I sell them.

I really liked the Army. I had all those years in. I was getting good pay. I knew I couldn't get that kind of pay outside. It was professionally rewarding. I tell you, I worked every department that there was in the military. I had been an OB nurse. I had been a surgical research nurse. I did research on burns. I had operating room, medical, everything. I consider myself an extremely well-rounded nurse because of Vietnam. I really thought that I was at the top of my career. I left the service because my mother had become ill. She had Alzheimer's disease. And I felt that I couldn't travel anymore. I didn't want to leave her. Although my sister is here, I didn't want to leave her. And I didn't want to go back into an operating room. First of all, I didn't think I could get along with the personnel. I couldn't. I found myself being extremely short-tempered when people tried to give me orders after I came back from Vietnam. I found myself getting extremely short-tempered at all this nonsense. So I felt, before I got court martialed, the best thing for me was to get out of the service.

Karen Bush

I went to nursing school at Columbia University in New York City. I wanted to go into the Army because it was an adventure. It was something I didn't think I could get anywhere else, certainly not the travel or the experience. And I wasn't crazy about taking care of geriatric patients. I figured in the Army I wouldn't have a whole lot of geriatric patients. My friends thought I was absolutely out of my gourd. Two friends of mine were particularly critical, I don't know why. They told me I was out of my mind, this is crazy. And I said, "Yeah, all right, it's my life." But after I came into the service, after about six months or so, I got a call from both of them and they had both joined the Air Force. They said, "We didn't know!" Well, they had gone to California, worked in a hospital there, and they said it was horrible. They couldn't meet anyone. People came to work, worked, and then went back to wherever they lived and that was it; and they had no opportunity to meet people except when they were at work. So they decided to try the Air Force.

I had no idea whether I'd make it a career or not. I didn't go into it with any preconceived notions. I assumed that it could turn into a career, but I did not set out for anything specific. I did not have the

Karen Bush served as a nurse with the 71st Evacuation Hospital in Pleiku in 1969 and 1970. Born in 1944, she grew up in Troy, New York. Bush is active in the Army reserves. A homemaker in San Antonio, she is a foster parent for the Texas Department of Human Services.

goal to get married or the goal to be a career officer. As a nurse I wanted hands-on experience in things that nurses couldn't do, that were illegal at that time in New York state at least. Nurses couldn't start IVs, and they couldn't draw blood. And so as nursing students we didn't do those things. I thought, well, I bet in the Army it's different. And it sure was. Working in a civilian hospital is not a thrilling experience, especially where I was working. This was the kind of situation where I was dealing with people who were mostly 65 or over. This is not thrilling. You may find them delightful, you may enjoy it . . . but it's not a thrill a minute. Vietnam was a thrill a minute. Most of the time, anyway.

After basic at Fort Sam Houston, they kept me in San Antonio at Brooke Army Medical Center. I worked in the recovery room and in the intensive care unit, both of which were attached to the general male surgical unit. This was where I met Gary, my future husband. He was a corpsman there. He was enlisted, a potential no-no. Well, it wasn't so bad during Vietnam because there were people who were enlisted who were far better qualified academically than some of the officers. So the separation of the enlisted (personnel) from the officers was not something that was really frowned upon. I mean it was not encouraged, but it was not discouraged either.

Anyway, he and I had worked together one night in the recovery room. It had been particularly hectic, and he said to me, "You're the most inefficient nurse that I have ever met in my entire life." I turned around and said, "What?" He said, "You want to go out for coffee?" "Sure, why not. It's only one in the morning. I can handle it," I answered. So we went out for coffee. He was dating a girl who had been transferred to Japan. And I had been dating a boy who was in New York. Misery loves company, right? I can't say we dated, because we didn't date in the sense that he would call me up and would say, "Listen I want to go out to dinner." We'd ride the train at Brackenridge Park in San Antonio. We'd go feed horses. When we were working evenings, we'd drive up to Bandera and back. And so we just sort of hung around together. We worked the same shifts and we enjoyed doing inexpensive things. I mean he couldn't afford to take me to La Louisianne and drive a Porsche.

I had my orders before he did. But he wound up going to Vietnam first. So I asked, "Well, what's going to happen to us?" He said,

"What do you mean?" "Well, if you go over there, are you going to write or what?" I asked. Because we really hadn't thought too much about getting married. Somewhere along the line he had decided that his girlfriend could stay in Japan and I had decided that my boyfriend could stay in New York. I had more in common with Gary than I did with this other guy. So there was no . . . I mean, he didn't get down on his knee and say, "Would you marry me?" It was just sort of understood that we would be married someday. We get along so well, we decided what the heck. I haven't found anybody better. He was 27 and I was 24 and so we decided we had done all our running and our carousing. We just didn't need to do that anymore.

I volunteered to go over. It was inevitable and I wanted to choose the time that I went rather than have them say, "You're going to go next month" or "You're going to go in six months," or whatever. Everyone was going. Besides I wanted to get the heck out of Brooke because they were running us ragged, working us 12 and 14 nights in a row, and we were on six days a week. We were grossly under-staffed and I just wanted a change. As far as Gary went, I thought at the time if this was something that was going to last or was real, then it would endure. Period. And if we were separated, we were sepa-rated. We would eventually get back. The thought of either of us dying never entered my mind. Well, I won't say that it didn't enter my mind. It went in one ear and out the other. There was no question in my mind that we were both going to survive.

It was possible to manipulate it so that you didn't go. But I thought that was a cop-out. I could probably have manipulated it so that I was at the right place at the right time. But in the first place, I had no idea how to do it; and in the second place, I did not think it was right. If you were in the Army and there was something going on, you had an obligation to go. Gary was out with the grunts as a medic. He doesn't think that his experiences are something that you should dwell on. The past is over, gone. There is very little that you can do about it, so you have to live in the present and go on. So he did not burden me with a lot of horror stories of things that he had done or things that he had seen. He didn't do that.

We got off the airplane in Vietnam and there were nine females together, which was something that was unusual at the time. That

many females never came over in one fell swoop. We got off the
airplane and people were screaming and cheering and everything. It
was a zoo. It was crazy. "You're here! Oh, we're so glad you're
here!" A major picked up my duffel bag for me. We were replacing
them. They were going home. So you see it wasn't all just the pleas-
ure of seeing American females. But still I'd never been greeted
like this before, let alone having a major whisk my duffel bag away.
And I remember riding on the bus from the airport to the compound
thinking, "Now remember all this." I looked at these huts and went
"Oh my God! Now remember this. Don't forget what it looks like
because you'll never be able to go back again. Just remember what
these things are like . . . this is a shanty town."

You lose a lot when you talk about Vietnam because you don't
have the smell. It's the smell of fish, nuc mam, and shit burners. I
don't know another nice word for it. That's the way you burn excrement with diesel fuel. There weren't many Army camps with sewer
systems over there. So the Army set up out-houses and you sat on
this board with a hole. Underneath there was a used 50-gallon drum,
and when that reached a certain level, they pulled it out and put in a
new one. Then they poured diesel fuel on this 50-gallon drum and
set it afire. They didn't just do one or two at a time. You'd see fields
of these things burning. Also the Vietnamese burned wood and
charcoal for cooking. All that in addition to the damp and the wet,
and the mold and the mildew. So it was all these smells combined.
Your senses were going "Holy Smoke!" And when you talk about it
and you see pictures of it, it loses something because you don't have
the smell.

The first night in Vietnam we spent in Long Binh. We went to the
officers club. There were nine of us. We went in and all the tables
were taken. The nine of us had just walked in and we all stood there.
I said, "This is not really terrific. I do not feel like standing here."
And suddenly it hit the men, "My God those are girls!" They started
clearing places, throwing chairs up in the air. It was a riot! There
must have been 200 people in that place. A moment before, they had
been sitting there drinking beer or whatever. Then they saw us and in
a minute they had cleared away a dance floor. And we danced, we all
danced until the 11 o'clock curfew. You danced with one fellow for
about two or three minutes, then somebody else would cut in and it

was like that. It was really funny to see their expressions, because they weren't used to women and all of a sudden here were all these females—it took awhile to sink in. It was a little sad, a little amusing . . . maybe a little of both. The morale just sky-rocketed. It was wonderful to watch. To see these people who were sitting there yacking with their buddies that they had been looking at for 20, 30, 40, 50, 60 days or longer, and then suddenly realize "My goodness, there's somebody else here." They'd slung their feet up with the mud and everything. But when we got there it changed a little bit, their social graces returned. The men enjoyed it. I never saw any of them again to my knowledge.

The assignment people at Long Binh asked me where I wanted to go. I asked them, "Where's the action? Where are things interesting?" They said, "Well, there's not much going on on the coast." There wasn't much going on anywhere on the coast during that period. But they said, "You know it's kind of busy in Pleiku." I said, "Fine. That's where I'll go." I knew Gary was up there in that area, but if they had said the action was someplace else I would have gone there. As it turned out, Gary's base camp was 15 miles away. But he was out in the field. He didn't come back in until August.

My introduction to Pleiku was to slip and fall in the mud, flat on my face. Just like that, and I'd been there less than an hour. Pleiku is all red clay and slippery and I just slipped and went sliding right on my face. It was wonderful! I said, "Oh boy, welcome to Vietnam." And of course the women giggled. Vietnamese women giggle when they get nervous or upset. I thought, "Oh, this is going to be terrific." I checked in at the headquarters at the hospital and found a message that Gary had been looking for me. He left messages everywhere. He'd been over there every day for weeks. I don't know how he found out I was coming to Pleiku. But he's real good at scrounging for things, including information.

I was assigned to ward number five. Ward number five was anything that wasn't surgery. We had hepatitis, malaria—lots of malaria—psych, ob-gyn, POWs, heart attacks, drug overdoses, venereal disease, dysentery. The overdose cases were the ones that got extremely violent. You couldn't get near them. One fellow had gotten out of his restraints and got hold of the little Vietnamese lady who cleaned, and he slammed her. She must have gone a good 20 feet. Then he ran out and they had to tackle him on the helipad. It took about five of them to get him under control. I don't know what had made him that way.

Lots of these people went off the deep end and went psychotic probably from very small things that wouldn't normally set anyone off, but it had been a combination or a result of incident upon incident that just triggered them off. One man came in and was so depressed, I had never seen anything like it. It was like every time I looked into his eyes, they were like pools getting deeper and deeper. They had called in artillery and they called it in wrong. It ended up right on top of their own people. He went to grab his friend and his friend's head rolled off. So he went crazy, which I thought was perfectly normal under the circumstances. But you couldn't get to him. There was no way you could reach him. You know, he just kept going deeper and deeper. I talked to him, asked him his name and anything that would have been sort of an automatic response—and there was nothing. I had dealt with depressed patients before, but not to this extent. And we were not equipped to deal with psychiatric patients. We didn't have a psychiatrist that I know of. Maybe we did, but I wasn't aware of one. A lot of the men who came to us were so terribly violent that you had to drug them right up to the limit. You couldn't get to them.

Relatively speaking our ward was very quiet. People did sleep at night. We didn't have that frantic constant running, treating sort of thing that went on in the surgical wards or in the emergency room. We did a lot of talking with the patients at night. The fellows couldn't sleep, so they'd come on up and sit down and we'd sit and yack about anything. We had one RN and one corpsman assigned during the night shift. I worked well with the corpsman. We had one poor boy who had dysentery something fierce, and he came up just trailing brown. I said to the corpsman, "Now you go in there and you clean him up. Because for me to clean him up in the middle of the night all by myself, it's going to be very awkward for him, and I don't want to put him in that kind of a situation." The corpsman thought that I should do the cleaning because it was "nursing stuff," and he should "swab the deck." Anyway, I went back and stripped the mattress off the bed, mopped the floor, and got him set up. That was the sort of activity that we had.

You could get drugs anywhere. You could buy them on the open market over there. They had a little white pill. I forget the name, but it had Demerol, morphine, cocaine. Anyway, it produced a predictable sequence of events after an overdose. When they came in they would be like a wet dishcloth. Then after a specific length of time they would become exceedingly violent. If they just had a simple overdose or were not addicted, then they would have a short recovery period. Now if they were addicted to the drugs, they would go through withdrawal and everything that goes with withdrawal— screaming, ranting, raving, kicking. I remember I got to talk to one such case who came in. I was so mad at him. He was a darling boy. He'd thrown a thermos at the television, and he hit me in the jaw and knocked me across the room. I wasn't hurt that bad. But after the drug had gone through its course, he came out one night and talked to me about what had gone on. And I said, "Now why did you do something that dumb? Because that was really dumb." He said, "Well, everybody else was doing it." See, he had shot up a barracks. Peer pressure over there was very, very high. Because you were dealing with a very young, vulnerable population. So if Joe Smith did it, well, hell, I can do it too. You know, that's the kind of man I am or that's the kind of person I am. So they would take this drug or any drugs and some of them would take this particular type of drug—I wish I knew the name—and they would become violent.

We were in a rear area, so we saw a lot of people doing things out of boredom. We had one young man who came in and he had been cohabitating with a female Vietnamese and she got pregnant. He very much wanted to marry her, but she wouldn't have anything to do with him. She did not want him. He went crazy, insane, hopping over eight-foot fences, I mean wild behavior. He slipped out of leather restraints, crawled down the middle of the ward, and it took several days to locate him. I had one young man who came in who was pretending to be crazy because he was so scared. He had not taken any drugs, he was just pretending to be crazy. I showed him one young man who had really gone psychotic because of what he had seen out in the field. And I said, "Now listen, you had better shape up or you're going to end up like that. You've got to pull yourself together." I don't know how I knew he was faking. There were all these things the doctors always called sub-clinical clues. You can't put your finger on what it is that makes you think something is wrong. But the doctors always say, "When the nurses say something isn't right, listen." Because it almost always turns out that something wasn't right. I don't know why I thought he was faking, because he was acting nutsy. It must have been something inconsistent in his behavior that didn't go along with what I had seen of those coming in from the field.

I was worried that if he continued to act crazy, he was going to really *be* crazy. I said to him, I said, "Now listen." I said, "You know you just have to kind of settle down here." I said, "Right now you're sane and you're going to have to compose yourself. And don't act crazy. You can be scared and urinate in your pants or whatever," I said. "Nobody's going to give two hoots and a holler if you do that, because everybody else is just as scared as you are. And to be scared isn't something that's bad. It's just a fact of life." It was giving him permission to be afraid. Acting crazy is acceptable. If you're crazy, people will accept that you're crazy and will accept that you're afraid. If you are a man, then you are not afraid. To be afraid is sissy. At least I suppose that's what he thought. He was bright, you know, he was not a fool. He was not stupid. So after about a week of his acting crazy I had had enough of it, and I told him he was going to have to stop.

He wasn't a danger to anyone. He kind of watched where he threw his arms. There wasn't this look in his eyes, the kind I'd seen in the guys who were really out of it. You see he'd never been out in the field. I said, "Now talk with some of the men who have been out in the field. Go around and talk to them and ask them." He'd never been there and he was scared. Hell, I don't blame him. He didn't feel it was right to be scared and so this was his way of coping and adjusting. So he went around and talked with some of the fellows who had been out in the field. Eventually he went to a unit, and I don't know what happened after that. You see there were a lot of loose ends. That's one thing about Vietnam that was very disconcerting. There were a lot of loose ends. You never knew what happened to these people. They went out and—who knows?

We had another patient we called "the recreational director." He came in very, very frightened. He was considered a psych patient. He was very, very frightened and exhibited all kinds of bizarre behavior. He could not be depended upon in the field. Exactly what he had done out there, I do not know. But he could not have been a backup for another man. He was just too frightened to be able to function. He was very verbal and you couldn't tell exactly what was wrong with him, other than that he was scared. And once he got into a safe environment where he didn't feel that his life was in danger at every second, he functioned very well. I think had he not been put in the field, had he been put into another area that was less life threatening, he probably could have functioned well. But because of where he was out in the field, he just couldn't function.

He was a real upbeat fellow when he was feeling safe. He was very concerned about the well-being of the patients who were on the ward. He was particularly sympathetic to the malaria patients who would get such high fevers. He was always getting them something to drink, getting soda from the Red Cross, buying it with his own money to bring to the men to make them feel better. He was a big help on the ward for the short time he was there. He was out of place in the field fighting. He should have been in the hospital where he really could have done a bang-up job. But there was no way of knowing in advance what level of stress he could take.

We sent him to Saigon where they had a psychiatric facility. Once again we never found out what happened to him. The feeling now is that when you have a psychiatric patient come in, you do intensive questioning and talking to him right there. In Vietnam that was not the case. We got the patients in, and they were medicated immediately. Because, for the most part, they were extremely violent; and then you just waited until they were air evac'd. We had not been trained in how to talk to the people who were psych patients. Many of them were in no condition to talk to anybody. I mean there was no way you could go into a room with a patient who was not medicated and expect to get anything out of him. They were terribly violent.

Once we had a guy in our ward, I think he was in there for malaria. He told us, "I don't know how the nurses stand it. I have never seen so much sickness and death and dying and gross mutilation as I have seen in this hospital, and I have been out in the field for almost a year." He said, "Somebody gets hit, poof, he's gone in a heli- copter." I don't know, I think that when people's friends were injured and went away or were evacuated or whatever, there was that loss there. It was almost as if they had died even if they hadn't. But I don't think they saw on an everyday basis all the things that we saw.

I was amazed at how routine war could become. It was frighten- ing. I mean I wasn't scared but it was frightening how routine it was—the skirmishes, guns going off all the time, alerts, the Cobras working off in the distance. It all became a matter of routine. The Cobras were gun ships and every fifth round, I think, was a tracer, and you could see them in the distance working over the areas where they thought the Viet Cong were. The first time I saw it, boy, was I impressed. You could see it from anywhere. It looked as if red satin ribbons were streaming from the helicopter.

The first time I was really frightened was when Gary and I went to town to get married. When a couple gets married in a foreign coun- try and both of the members are in the service, they have to be married under the provisions of that country. In Vietnam, this meant going down to the town hall and posting your names, and then 10 days later going back and signing your name again. They did not require any kind of religious ceremony, although you could have one. We went downtown—me, Gary, and a driver. I had an M-16. You could not leave anything in your vehicle because it would be taken. So we chained the vehicle down, then we were suddenly sur- rounded by all these children. And all I could think of was "My God, who's going to throw the grenade?" I was petrified, absolutely petrified. We walked in and we signed our names, and I was scared to death because I thought this was it. I'm dead.

You could never tell how old these children were. They were very small. By our standards it was very difficult to determine the ages of the children. Somebody who was 14 might look seven to me. I had no idea of how to estimate the ages of these children. And so I was frightened. I thought, "God, if I have to shoot these kids I'm going to die." But I also thought, "Well if it's them or me, by God, it's not going to be me." I had just set my mind that way. But I would not have found it an easy thing to do.

And then one other time I was scared to death. I was so frightened. We had been in Saigon. We had gotten one of those pedi-cabs. We told them we wanted to go to Tan Son Nhut. We found ourselves in some slum somewhere with pigs and mud puddles. I thought, "This is it." We had cameras . . . that was the extent of our defense. And I thought "We're dead. We are dead." Or at least Gary's dead and I'm captured. Because that would have been wonderful. A wonderful hostage situation. That was something we were always mindful of.

Some of the nurses had wanted to get combat medic badges, not just the medical badge. But in order to do that, you had to spend two weeks on a fire base. So we said we wanted to go out to a fire base to spend two weeks. The administrators said "No" and I asked "Why?" They said, "Well, you might be killed;" and I said, "That's not the reason. What's the reason?" "Well, we don't want you to get captured." They said it would be impossible to negotiate. And that the men wouldn't put up with it because I was a woman. The Viet Cong would have had the upper hand, they could have negotiated anything. But if the United States had said "Kill them," the men would not have taken kindly to that. There would have been a real problem.

The most interesting contact I had with the Vietnamese outside the hospital was with the Montagnard tribesmen. They are a small, brown people who are all muscle. They wear very little clothing. The women wear long black, wrap-around skirts from the waist to the ankle. They're nude from the waist up. They smell like smoke all over. The men wear loin cloths and no shoes. The women urinate standing up, which is a sight to behold. Whew, such control! They loved the Americans because the Americans always treated them very well. They were loyal to the Americans, so it was a two-way street. When they were brought into the hospital, they were always on their very best behavior. They chewed betel nut and they spit. So we used to get tape tubes—tape comes in tubes—so we taped them onto the bed so they could spit into them, instead of on the floor. But they were always on their very best behavior. For the most part, they all got well. In instances where they could not be saved, their people would take them home. They believed that if you died outside your village your soul wandered. They never went to the hospital by themselves. You could tell their families, or whoever, how to put up a second or a third IV depending on how long it was going to take them to get back to their village. And then they would take these people with their IVs back to the village to die. That was respected. The hospital did not insist that we keep them there until they died.

They were simple mountain people, basically nomads and hunters. Since we were in the Highlands, we went out on medcaps to their villages to give them medical care. For many of them, I was the only white female they had ever seen. One little kid came zipping around a hut and took one look at me and screamed bloody murder, and went zipping back. You know, like, "God, what kind of person is this?" There was one man who we thought had chicken pox, but actually it turned out to be smallpox. It manifested itself differently over there. We had to bribe them with Kool-aid drinks in order to get them to be immunized. We did this in four villages, and one thing that I thought was really interesting was that even though there were three of us doing immunizations, all the females came to me because I was the only female. It didn't matter if I was strange and threatening.

The Viet Cong dealt ruthlessly with the Montagnard. They mutilated one little boy—we got him with his arm hanging by a tendon. He was only nine. Another gal had one breast whacked off—a young girl. Just awful stuff. I mean they didn't have the decency to kill these people. They just left them there in their devastated village to die this horrible death.

All the time I was in Pleiku, I never worried about Gary. I never did. He's a survivor. I was never afraid. Maybe it was just stupidity. Maybe it was youth. Maybe it was never having been through this before. I don't know. But I was never afraid that he would not come back. Maybe I supressed it, hell, I don't know. I was never consciously afraid he would not come back. Now I thought it more of a comfort to have him around, of course, especially when I was brand new in country, because people wouldn't talk to me. It was very difficult. And to have someone just to pass the time of day with was very nice.

The moral standards of fellow Americans was not a topic that we discussed much. I do know that there were a group of girls in one hooch who seemed to be a little more lax in their moral standards, shall we say, than others. There were lines at the back of the hooch. I hesitate to say anything because under the circumstances it might not have been such a bad idea. War makes strange bedfellows and that's the truth. And if this is a way they found that they could cope and maintain their sanity or their feelings that someone cared for them, well heck, it was all right by me. It was lonely. I don't care who you were, it was lonely.

Gary had sent me a ring, a PX special from Vietnam, while I was still in the states. So I thought, "Wow." I went to see if it was real. I went to a jeweler to see if it was a real diamond. It was, and so I figured he was serious. I didn't tell my parents, though. Because I figured that just would have been more than they could handle at that point. They were having a hard time with my going to Vietnam, let alone my getting married. But we had already decided by the time I got there. We might have waited to get back to the states to get married, but I got pregnant. I can pinpoint it—I got pregnant on the 17th of August between four and six in the afternoon. Someone asked, "How do you know?" And I said, "You just know!" We wanted to get married, but they kept holding up our paperwork for almost three months. It was like my father would have said, "You got knocked up." I wanted to go out to a Montagnard village. I was going to fly out and Gary said—it was so funny, it was before we were married—"You can't go out there. You're pregnant!" I said, "The hell I can't. I can so. We're not married yet, fellah." And then it was that I couldn't go to Hong Kong on R&R. "You can't go to Hong Kong, you're pregnant." I said, "Tough."

I had real mixed emotions when I found out that I was pregnant. Because I really did want to be pregnant, but I really wanted to stay and complete my tour. And I felt "Gee whiz, I can be pregnant and complete my tour with no problem." I did not want to be there under false pretenses. I told my superiors. I said that I wanted to stay, that I did not feel a pregnant female was a sick female, and that I would not hold the Army responsible for the child. The net result was that they gave me 21 hours notice to get out. I was very angry because I did not feel that my pregnancy was a factor in my performance. I'd been pregnant since August, and this was January already. I did not feel that my pregnancy had . . . well, it had had some impact because I was a little draggy. But when you're working 12 hours a day, anybody gets a little draggy.

After Vietnam, I went to Walter Reed Army Hospital to get discharged, and then I went on leave to visit my parents. Gary was still in the Army and we were stationed at Fort Hood for a year. Then the Army sent him back to Vietnam. This time he was in the Delta. His position there was a lot more tenuous than it had been before. He was with the Kit Carson scouts. But he got out of that within several months, because he didn't feel that the scouts were to be trusted. It was just not a real nice situation to be in. So he became a member of a team that went out into different areas. These were five-man teams. They taught defense to the natives in these areas, and they went out on patrols and that sort of thing. I went back to upstate New York to stay near my parents, which I wouldn't do again because I found myself becoming very dependent upon them. It wasn't so much out of desire as out of necessity. I lived in my hometown and I didn't know anybody. Everybody I knew was gone.

I didn't do any nursing after Vietnam because I had Christopher. I wanted to join the reserves when we were at Fort Hood, and Gary said no. And of course I, thinking that you had to be a docile little wife, went along with his wishes. After I had been on my own for a year while he was in Vietnam, I thought, "Well, heck." So after he came back I approached him again about going into the reserves, because I had always felt a little guilty that I had not completed my obligation. The Army had helped finance my last year in nursing school, and I really felt guilty about that. It was something that I didn't like leaving undone. I put it to Gary in those terms, and he said, "You really want to do it?" I said, "Yeah, I really do." Then he said OK.

The reason I didn't work after I came back was not because I was soured against nursing. It was a question of priorities. For me, staying home and raising a family was more important than working in nursing. I try to stay as current as I can. I can't possibly stay up to date on everything. Being in the reserves was also another way of keeping my finger in the pie. Also I work on a volunteer basis in the hospital. My interest in it has never really lessened.

I think the impact that Vietnam had on most people is grossly overstated. "Well, you don't have children because you were in Vietnam," or "You take care of foster children because you were in Vietnam," or "You're divorced because you were in Vietnam," or "You've been married for 15 years, that's because you were in Vietnam," . . . I think that's a lot of nonsense. I think that proportionally speaking, the veterans who were crazy, the ones who are divorced, the ones who are long-married, the ones who have families, the ones who do not have families—all these are probably not any greater than the general population. The explosive Enquirer-type stories make me very angry. These are very, very few people in proportion to the numbers of people who were over there.

For me, having a family is my full-time job. When I took the career course as part of my reserve training, I discovered that I was not good at having a career and having a family. I did not feel I was doing well. I could not give the time and the effort to either that I wanted to give. And if I want to do something, I want to do it well. For me to work and have a family is not doing my best.

My parents were very supportive of me when I went over there. I always felt that if there was no one else in the world I could talk to, I could always talk to them—even if I hadn't had Gary. I would never ever have given up the experience of going over, because when I got back I was a far better nurse than I could have ever hoped to be had I stayed in the states. It didn't matter whether I was going to pursue a career actively or not. The point was that I found I could function far better than any of my counterparts who had never been over there. I was not threatened by the physicians because I had been a co-worker, I had not been a subordinate. I had no compunctions about walking into a circle of doctors and stamping my foot and saying, "Now we have to get organized here, fellows, because you're going in 14 directions, and we need to get some organization in this patient's care." This did not bother me. A number of the other nurses, who had not had the experience I had, thought it was very difficult to confront a group of physicians. That's because they had always played a subordinate role. I felt "Hell, I've been through a lot more than you guys have, and if you can't handle it, I can."

Deanna McGookin

I decided to come into the Army in 1968 primarily because I had quite a bit of emergency room experience from working at Maricopa County Hospital in Phoenix. I had also worked several emergency rooms in Los Angeles County. There was a big push on to recruit nurses at that time. I came in with the guarantee of assignment to Vietnam, because that is what I wanted to do. I worked in an emergency room (in an area) where there were a lot of arguments and quarrels settled by violence. On a Saturday evening it was not untypical at all to treat two or three gunshot wounds or several stabbings. And I used to think that that particular method of solving arguments was useless, futile, didn't solve anything, but ruined already disturbed family units. I thought I had a skill I had developed over the years. I felt that although I did not totally agree with our being in Vietnam for the reasons we were, I had something I could provide the GIs. And I felt that the service I could provide them was, for me, more valuable than what I was giving to people who were deliberately harming each other. I was dealing with people who were slicing each other up, shooting each other, and it didn't seem to matter if they were friends, family, or whatever. I felt I

Lt. Col. Deanna McGookin served at the 67th Evacuation Hospital in Qui Nhon from October, 1968 to October, 1969. Born in 1941 in Canada, she grew up in Phoenix, eventually obtaining American citizenship. She has been in the Army 19 years, serving at a number of posts abroad and in the United States. She is currently Chief of the Department of Nursing, Kenner Army Community Hospital, Fort Lee, Virginia.

could help the GIs best with the skills that I had developed—emergency life-support care. I knew that a nurse working rapidly and efficiently could make a big difference.

I kept hearing in the news about how they were able to air evacuate the soldiers, getting them home in such short time. Within 48 hours of his injury, a soldier could be in a hospital close to his home. So I felt that kind of work was more significant than working in the county hospital emergency room. The GIs were serving their country as they were asked to do, and I felt the least I could do was go over there and provide them the best nursing support possible. I had fully intended to get out after that initial tour of duty, but the Army provided me with what I wanted out of nursing. I grew to appreciate the type of medical care given in the military and decided to stay on. Of course, the years accrue and you get yourself hooked on it after awhile.

I was 27 at the time I came in. I was the oldest of three girls. We had moved to Arizona from Canada for health reasons. My mother had a chronic illness. My father had served in the Canadian Army in World War II, but never overseas. Being a naturalized citizen may have made me a more intense patriot than I otherwise might have been. It's like a new convert to a religion. My father used to feel kind of relieved he had all daughters, so there'd be no possibility he'd have to send children to war. But I really felt I had a kind of service to perform. I enjoyed being able to do what I could for people who, through no fault of their own, found themselves in life-threatening situations. At that time, the civilian emergency room was not at the skill level we see nowadays. I had a friend whose husband was retired military, and he kind of put the bug in my ear so to speak—the opportunities to travel, that kind of thing. That was another reason why I was looking at the possibility. I talked to recruiters from the Air Force and Army, and decided to go into the Army because their opportunities seemed better. I liked the places where I could be stationed. The Air Force bases seemed scattered away from cities.

I spent my year in Vietnam at the 67th evac in Qui Nhon, which was the headquarters of II Corps. The conditions were pretty much what I expected—but not the bulk, the quantity of wounded. In Phoenix, we were used to seeing one or two come in at a time. Now you were talking 50 or 60 at a time, with a wide variety of traumatic wounds. I had seen traumatic amputations of extremities from cotton picking combines in Arizona. So that was not a horrendous sight for me, as it was for some others. The bulk . . . that there were just so many of them coming in at once . . . that was the issue for me. You had these helicopters land and there could be 60–70 casualties with various stages of injuries. Some of them might not have been as serious as others. It depended on the season. In Tet of '69 we were getting 200–300 patients coming in a day.

I worked mainly in the emergency room and triage area. That's where you do life-saving procedures before sending them into the operating room. I literally picked them up off the helicopter or the ambulances, and brought them into the emergency room, and stabilized them as best I could before the operating room. The expectant category, that was the hardest. We are taught, trained, and socially groomed as nurses that every life is important. Your job as a nurse is to try to save human life to whatever extent possible. So when casualties were coming in fast and furious, and someone came in with such extensive injuries . . . what you'd be doing is sacrificing this one life who's expected to die anyway, and doing something for three or four others who could be saved. That was hard. Usually the nurses would have to sort out the wounded with a physician at hand. Some physicians were doing procedures to the patients, while still others were preparing for casualties in the operating room. But we always managed to keep them comfortable as far as medications were concerned.

We assigned a corpsman to each expectant so they wouldn't be by themselves. That was a hang-up on my part. I didn't like the idea of their being by themselves at that time. And whether they knew anyone was there or not, I always made sure someone was. At least there would be another human being. If they were in the expectant category, most often they could not communicate with anybody. Usually the only ones you put in expectant were the ones who had massive, open chest wounds with so much blood and body fluid lost that they were unconscious anyway. Or they had massive head injuries. Anything else, they went to the operating room and the surgeons there tried, to the best of their ability, to help them pull through. Although the expectants generally were comatose, one

would occasionally grab your hand. You could never know with
those folks whether they could hear you or not. The worst of the
other non-expectant ones were the traumatic amputations of legs or
other limbs. These had suffered tremendous blood loss, but there
was always a wait for donor-specific transfusions. It took 45 minutes
or so before they could have the blood typed and crossed and have it
ready by the time they were taken into the OR. So most were trans-
fused with O-negative before the crossmatch was complete. There
was a tremendous blood loss, tremendous fluid loss, and there was
some concern as to whether they'd make it or not.

When I think back to individual cases I saw coming through
there, I'm very much aware of this one young man. Ours was like
the dropping off point, we had the major air field at Qui Nhon. Men
were coming up to go to the 1st Division or the 173rd Infantry. So
they were arriving and their units came down to pick them up. There
was one young man, he was very small and blonde. And it was
obvious he hadn't shaved yet, because he was probably of Scandina-
vian origin; but he was very short and very blonde and I kept thinking how awfully young he looked. He'd stopped me to ask directions
to the Red Cross, because he wanted to call his mother back in the
states and tell her that he had just arrived. So his unit came and
picked him up and three days later he came back into the emergency
room with both his legs blown off. He had stepped on a land mine.
He was awake and he remembered me. I called him by name, his
name was Mark. I still remember that. He just looked up at me and
put his arms around my neck and pulled me down saying, "Please
don't let me die." And that was very hard. It was particularly difficult because he happened to be one of a large number coming into
the emergency room. There were about 60–70 coming in at the
same time. I told him, "We'll certainly do our level best," and I
stayed with him. Although I was head nurse of the emergency room,
I did my best to stay with him until he went to the operating room.
His right leg was six inches from the hip, the left was four inches
above the knee. There was no part left. Both legs had been totally
obliterated. The medic in the field had medicated him, so he was
conscious and reasonably comfortable until you moved him. Then
the pain became exaggerated. He was semi-conscious and his vital
signs were weak. The medic had put IVs in both arms which kept

him from bleeding to death.

Fortunately, he did survive the surgery and made it back to the states. And I understand, from the best I was able to keep up, that he did fairly well. Now how he managed as far as adjusting to life was concerned, I don't know. But he survived. He spent about two hours there in the emergency room talking to me while waiting for the jeep to come down and pick him up. He was drafted right out of high school. He had been an exceptional student in school, and had intended to go to medical school after he finished his commitment. He was going to go to the University of Michigan—he was from Grand Rapids—and go to medical school afterward. This was his goal in life. Who knows, maybe he would have been the individual who found the cure for some disease that is giving us so much of a problem.

Some died in the field, and we never saw those. They brought them back in body bags to Qui Nhon. We'd have them brought to us with the tags on them. It was an eerie thing to see a name you recognized in a big, black body bag. We had dozens more who came in with all sorts of injuries. One had wounds to the chest, we put chest tubes in him. He also survived. One came in, he had a massive face injury. He did not make it into the operating room. We had a very excellent oral surgeon who attempted to tie up the major vessels to get him through, but he had almost the full side of his face blown off. His buddy in front of him stepped on a mine. When you stepped on a mine, all you did was arm it. It's when you stepped off of it that you had the problem. His buddy who stepped on it didn't hear it click. When he stepped off of it, it exploded and the guy behind him got it in the face. He died in the emergency room.

We all had questions as to what we were doing in Vietnam, why we were there. We didn't seem to be getting anywhere. Day after day, things seemed to be pretty much the same . . . they'd take a hill, lose a hill, take a hill, lose a hill. Being in the age group where motherhood and children were a big factor, I think you do think: "What are we doing to the future generations of this country? What sort of genius would this blond young man have been had he been allowed to go about his life and do his own thing?" Most of the time you were so busy, just literally, physically busy that—although these thoughts stayed with you for awhile—you soon forgot about them, because it always seemed like there was someone else coming in to take the previous patient's place. Only when you got attached and knew someone before they got injured did it really bother you, as was the case with Mark.

It wasn't so depressing all the time, I must admit. We went on medcaps, medical missions to remote villages, places where there was no regular medical care. We did reconstructive surgery on children, gave them false limbs, and taught them how to get around. These kinds of things helped relieve some of the frustrations I was feeling. Some things that bothered the other people bothered me less. Seeing children with napalm burns, for instance. The reason it didn't bother me was that I saw children in Phoenix who had been shot by their fathers for no other reason than that the fathers were angry with the mothers. I had resolved that a long time ago. The children happened to be innocent bystanders. I'm not saying it's right. It's tragic, but it happens. It's unfortunate. Another thing was that Phoenix was the major source of napalm used in the bombs. There was a big chemical plant nearby. So we'd get burn patients when there'd be an accident at the napalm factory. I was used to treating napalm wounds, probably one of the few nurses in Vietnam with prior experience of this kind. You worked hard to restore them to their maximum health so they could carry on with their lives. It made very little sense, but at least I had already taken care of that in my personal life back in the emergency ward; so that when I got to Vietnam I could concentrate on restoring that child back to health as much as possible.

When you're over there you develop a tremendous camaraderie with everyone around you. For the most part you were confined to the compound. It wasn't until I got home that I had problems dealing with my having been in Vietnam, because the radio and TV in Vietnam kept us in the dark about a lot of the hostile feeling back home. When I came back, I mean people were absolutely, totally indifferent. Kids who I grew up with, went to nurse training with . . . they were outright hostile. They'd say, "It was a stupid war, we had no business being there," which is true. No one is saying we had a right to be there, but we were. We were committed. I think the biggest thing was their absolute, total indifference. The church my family belonged to was a great one for potluck dinners. So when I came back they had a potluck to welcome me back. There were very few people that mentioned anything about Vietnam. They didn't want to know anything about it. For someone coming back from an experience like that, the most important thing to do is talk about it. So what you did was you found someone who had been there and you talked about it with them. The news . . . it was unbelievable. People were running off to Canada and running off to everywhere else, and I'm not saying that's wrong. If that was their personal conviction they had a right to it. These people were getting played up. Shortly after, they gave amnesty to all those who went to Canada. But to the Vietnam veteran coming home, there was nothing. My first assignment after coming home was Fort Dix, N.J. There were GIs coming back with extremities missing, and they weren't given anything.

Everyone I knew in the Army nursing corps had either just come back from Vietnam or were just going. So we talked about it among ourselves. And whatever was necessary . . . if someone had a concern we'd just listen. We could appreciate it because we were there. I personally never saw anyone who had major difficulty with it. Some had problems initially because of the indifference of family . . . especially with the nurses because we were not in combat; and the men kept those hospitals secure, I assure you, because they knew that was where their lives could be won or lost. I know sometimes I was angry with the lack of recognition given the females, because we also spent a year there. I think this has since improved significantly. It's beginning to filter out that, yes, women served in Vietnam, too.

Was it, all told, a positive or negative experience? There was a lot of both. I don't think one negates the other. I grew up a lot and don't think . . . I'm still very angry at the response the country gave, not so much for myself but for some of these vets who had permanent disabilities. But it was definitely a growing experience, there were a lot of positive things that came out for myself, and that's the only one I can speak for. And there are a lot of things I'll carry around that make me very angry. I think sometimes the decisions that were made were not the best. But I realized as part of my own maturing process that not all decisions are the very best. I think I'm angry that those young blonde-haired, blue-eyed men didn't have a chance to finish their lives. I think everyone should have that chance. A lot of my resolving of personal conflict happened before I went over there, because I felt, for instance, that what was happening in Watts was totally insane. In Vietnam, we were—even if it was just on paper—attempting to free this nation for those who wanted to live in a democracy. What I was seeing in Watts, there was no sense to it.

As far as drugs, alcohol, sex—that sort of thing—let me say this: There wasn't any more of that there than there is here or anywhere where people gather together. Maybe per individual there was more alcohol consumed, but you have to remember we were confined to the compound and water was terrible. For the most part it was potable, but not palatable. So what you drank was soda water; and when Coke ate your stomach, you began to go to beer. Beer, by the way, is considered by many physicians to be the best diuretic you could use. You were actually encouraged to drink beer. As far as drugs and alcohol, it was no worse than what you see in any high school or any adult group across the country.

After I came home, I looked around and decided I didn't want to go back to Phoenix. I looked around at the salaries and job opportunities, even the possibility of going to New York City. I decided with what I had, the advantages the military offered to me, the opportunities for education, the opportunities to travel—because I do not like to stay very long in one place—that I'd stay in. In any case, civilian hospitals aren't too thrilled with nurses who come to work for them who have resumes that are three pages long because they bounced around. The military gave me the opportunity to do that without seeming undependable. It also gave me some benefits, and some structure. I thought several times about getting out since, but once you hit that 10-year mark, you're sort of locked in.

The military is definitely not for everyone. The Army used to prohibit marriages, and after that was overturned, they prohibited children. You used to have to wait your turn on education, and some nurses got out because they didn't want to wait. I like autonomy. When I worked as a civilian, frequently we were told which physicians we had to stand up for when they walked in the room. That's a bunch of baloney, as far as I'm concerned. In the Army, we are listened to, for the most part, by physicians. We carry rank on our shoulders, like physicians. We are more their equal than their adversary, which sometimes occurs in the civilian community. There's more of a team effort in military medicine. You don't have those nurse-doctor feuds you see so much in civilian hospitals, and I like that. I think I have enough experience, especially with interns, to be able to say to them "that's not right, you might want to look at this way." I have the experience, they don't. I also carry the authority to do that. In civilian hospitals, you can't. A doctor is a doctor is a doctor. It's difficult, you sometimes have to go in the back door, negotiate, approach it from another angle. That's not right if the patient loses in the long run. I like the idea of being able to be heard and being respected for the knowledge I've accummulated over the years.

After Vietnam, it was difficult for me to come back and allow someone with less experience to take over the responsibilities which had been mine—putting in chest tubes, for instance. But it's also one of the major reasons I decided to stay in the military—I had had civilian experience and military nurses are certainly allowed to do more than civilian nurses. I asked myself how much more would I feel that way if I went back into the civilian community? Because you can't even give an aspirin without a physician's order, you can't draw blood without a physician's order. Nursing was something I always wanted to do. I knew I had something to offer. More recently, I've thought about giving it up, because my 20-year mark in the service is approaching. But I cannot say that I thought of giving it up at that time. I worked in seven hospitals between age 21 and 27 before coming in service. I happen to like new challenges. That part of my personality existed before Vietnam.

When I came home to Phoenix the first time, the young boy down the block had a car that backfired all the time. Every time it backfired, I was on the floor and under the bed. And I'm still absolutely, positively terrified of weapons. They send me up to the rifle range and I'll do it. It's a personal challenge to me not to get too uncomfortable, so at least I can handle it; but I'm absolutely terrified of that M-16.

You hear such negative things about folks returning from Vietnam. I'm not saying people weren't traumatized and I'm not putting those folks down, but for the most part the biggest majority came home and were able to carry on with their lives the best they could. For the longest time, you seldom heard positive things about veterans, male or female. I think it would be more balanced if, for a change, we heard something about the folks who were there and who have come back and carried on their lives.

I think when we first went into Vietnam, our intentions were appropriate. But it seemed like once we got the foot in the door, the politics from both sides and the pressures from the population here in this country caused the whole situation to escalate out of control. I don't think the individuals initially involved in the decision ever imagined it would go on to the extent it did. I think it was sort of one of those things that evolved. Looking back on it, it seems like a useless effort. But, now having read something about how decisions were made, I do not think we had any idea what we were getting ourselves into. The politics got a little out of hand and that's where we ran amuck, so to speak. The way we had to get out of it was very stressful, I think, for those of us who were there. It was sad to see us walk out of the country, leaving everything. Now it is as bad if not worse than it would have been had we not walked in there in the first place.

Oh, we could have won the war, absolutely. There's no doubt that we had the firepower to do it, but that level of involvement might have escalated us into a world war. But who knows, because it never happened. The problem was that it was not the kind of war we were prepared to fight. These guys were swinging through trees with axes, so to speak. If you drop a bomb in an environment like that, you're going to kill your own men. We could have won, but the price would have been too high. We would have had universal world involvement before we got out, China and Russia. The price of continuing would have been too great.

I think things began to change for the veteran once they opened the Vietnam memorial in Washington. It's a formal recognition that "Yes indeed, we were involved in a conflict, whether popular or unpopular. And we do recognize that a lot of people lost their lives, and we do recognize that a lot of hard feelings have occurred. And that whatever else, this is the nation saying 'we do recognize you for the job you did.'"

It's almost as though the country is saying it's sorry that the whole

situation has occurred. Most of the young kids, the college genera-
tion, they don't know what Vietnam is all about. But for those of us
who experienced the war, we learned a lot, we really did. I learned a
lot about myself and what I could handle. I could handle a lot more
than I thought I could. I came from a very protected household. My
father had three daughters and there was nothing he didn't do for us.
We were provided with our education, all our needs. We were very
fortunate children. I was very lucky, and I came to realize how much
I could handle. There will probably be a breaking point out there for
me, somewhere . . . there is for all of us. But for right now anyway,
Vietnam taught me I was capable, pretty much, of handling anything.

Shirley Menard

I was 21 when I joined the Army. Well, actually, that's wrong, because I joined as a student nurse, so I was 19 or 20 when I joined; and as soon as I graduated, I worked for awhile in a civilian hospital while I was waiting for state board results. As soon as I got those, I was immediately assigned. I think I went down to Fort Sam Houston for basic training the third week in January, 1964. I was born in Lancaster, Pennsylvania, and grew up in Lititz, which is a small town right outside Lancaster—very famous for their Dutch pretzels and candy. Sturgis pretzels and Wilbur Suchard chocolates. A very famous town! I went to Bryn Mawr Hospital outside Philadelphia for my nurse's training. It was a three-year diploma program. I had an unhappy romance and bounced back by joining the Army. That was around 1962, so Vietnam was not in the news. We had just had the Bay of Pigs in Cuba and there was all this heightened military type stuff, and I said, "Hey, that's for me. I'm going to join the Army." And that's what I did. I was heartbroken so I joined the Army. I think the guys are supposed to do that, aren't they? I did it the other way around.

Born in Lancaster, Pennsylvania, in 1943, Shirley Menard served in the 8th Field Hospital in Nha Trang in 1966. She left the Army in 1968. Menard is an assistant professor at the University of Texas Health Science Center School of Nursing and a pediatric clinical nursing specialist at Medical Center Hospital in San Antonio. She is enrolled in a doctoral program at the University of Texas in Austin.

Joining as a student nurse meant that I committed two years of my life to the military for which they paid my last year of nurse's training. I graduated in September of '63 and worked for awhile at the hospital in Bryn Mawr while I was waiting for state board results. It takes about three to four months to get the state board results. And once I learned I had passed, I immediately heard from the military and they said to report to Fort Sam Houston. It was the last week of January, I believe, or like the 20th of January for basic training. That was the first time I had ever gone anywhere outside of Pennsylvania, other than once when I was like five years old, we had gone to Mississippi on a car trip. But I'd never been further than the Jersey shore. I went to New York City once with my high school class and that was a big thing.

It was a major event, leaving home for the Army. I remember it was my first airplane ride. It was an Eastern airplane and I remember we landed in Dallas—'cause it was ice cold when I left Pennsylvania, snowing, and my parents waving good bye, 'cause you didn't have those covered walkways then to go to the plane. You walked outside and up into the plane. And I had worn a wool dress with a heavy wool coat over it—it was snowing—boots, the whole bit. I got on the plane, my parents were waving good-bye. We landed in Dallas and it was chilly in Dallas, but not cold 'cause this was January. I got back on a two prop plane. We landed in San Antonio at the airport and I had this wool dress on—and it was like 88 degrees! The sun was shining, it was gorgeous. I was so sweaty and miserable. There were four or five of us who had arrived early for basic. February 11th sticks in my mind as the day I was commissioned. And that meant that we were able to go to work. So they sent us to work in the military hospital there at Fort Sam Houston. I worked at Beach Pavilion. And I was assigned to an ENT, which is Ear, Nose, and Throat ward. At that time the Ear, Nose, and Throat ward had a lot of patients with cancer. They all had had tracheostomies. I walked up onto the ward my first day in my little white uniform and my white Army hat and the whole bit, brand new second lieutenant. I walked into the ward and I passed by this bed and this first guy says, "Well, about time we got some pretty nurses up here." And I looked down and here's this guy laying there with his face all messed up, a trach and NG tubes, and I said, "Is this what I'm in the Army for?" And he was kind of winking at me, so I just kept walking to report to the head nurse to begin my duties. And this guy kept tagging after me. Well, as it turned out, that was my husband-to-be. The first person I met in an Army hospital, and he was my first patient.

He'd been in an accident and one side of his face was just smashed, and all the ribs on one side were broken. He'd been in intensive care for five days. He was really messed up. They didn't expect him to live. So he'd been in the hospital at that time for quite awhile. He was better, but not well enough to leave yet. Anyway, he kept following around after me and he would talk to me. Of course, in a military hospital it's a little bit different than a civilian hospital. The patients do a lot of the work. They make their own beds, they look after other patients because there are not as many hospital personnel assigned, at least at that time. So he would follow around and he'd bring coffee and that kind of stuff, and we got to talking. Well, time went by and when he was discharged he asked me if I would like to go out. At that time I didn't realize you weren't supposed to date enlisted men. I mean nobody had told me you weren't supposed to date enlisted men. I didn't know, so I said, "sure."

So we started dating. It was really funny 'cause we'd have to be real secretive about it. I'd drive my car to the Post Exchange and he'd drive his car to the Post Exchange, and we'd meet there. We'd look around, making sure the coast was clear, and I'd go with him for a date and then he'd drop me off back at the PX. I'd pick my car up and go on back to the bachelor officer's quarters. San Antonio was a very small town, even coming from rural Pennsylvania. There wasn't a lot to do. There was the zoo, the Alamo, Brackenridge Park, the river, the boats, and all that kind of stuff. We went dancing a lot. We would drive to Fredericksburg for a barbecue dinner. We'd go to The Chatter Box. And at that time for $1.50 you could get a T-Bone steak that covered the plate, french fries and garlic bread, salad and ice tea. You got to pick your own steak. We went to the drive-in, to the movies, the drag races—San Antonio Drag Races were there.

In the military, at that time, you not only didn't date enlisted men, I mean you didn't get married. It was not considered appropriate for nurses to be married at that time. There was an old-fashioned rule that your number one priority was to nursing in the military. And that's OK, but by their way of thinking this meant that you didn't have a separate life, because it might mean your priorities weren't the same as the military's. It was not unusual to be stationed apart from your husband if you did get married. They did not make very much effort to station you together. That's changed. I think today they do try to keep you together if you're married. But it hasn't changed much as far as officer/enlisted relationships. And I can understand some of that. I think if you're working together in the same place, you're an officer and your husband is enlisted, and you're in charge of the floor that he's working on, that it would be very difficult to discipline. I mean I could understand that. But my husband had nothing to do with medicine. He was a mess sergeant and he worked in the mess hall. And not even in the hospital mess hall. He was assigned to a different company, but he was stationed at Fort Sam. So, for us, there was no conflict.

We dated, I guess, starting in April, and by May he had already asked me to marry him. I thought about it. I was supposed to go to Denver, Colorado, to Fitzsimmons Army Hospital. On the last day of my basic training there was a recruiter there who asked if anyone would please want to get their assignments changed to Fort Sam Houston, that they really needed nurses to stay at Fort Sam. Well, my arm was first up in the air, because of my husband-to-be. So I stayed at Fort Sam and went to work at Beach Pavilion. I went home on leave after basic training. Actually I drove my husband's car home—we weren't married yet—I drove my boyfriend's car home and he kept mine in San Antonio while I drove his, only because his was a larger car. And there were four of us heading for Pennsylvania. And then I brought my mother back with me from Pennsylvania and she met him, and we dated through the summer and got married in October.

It was really kind of funny, we had decided to get married, but we didn't want to set a date because he was on maneuvers, getting called on duty at different times. It all may have had something to do with Vietnam, because Vietnam was beginning to build up. Not a big buildup, but there were these little rumors going around, and we started receiving a few casualties in the hospital from some of the special forces troops that were there as advisers. They had been ambushed. At Fort Sam, at that time, there were always these weekend-type jaunts to Camp Bullis, going out into the Texas wilderness for training or whatever. And you never knew when they were going to pull one. So after our first attempt at getting married had been aborted by one of these, we decided that the first weekend when we were free together, we were just going to go get married. That weekend turned out to be October 31, Halloween, of '64. So we ran off to Seguin and got married. And the reason we ran off to Seguin was because at that time it was the only place in Texas close by where you could get married without a waiting period. San Antonio had a three-day waiting period. So we just went to Seguin one Saturday morning, October 31, and got married at the courthouse.

The casualties, the extremely remote possibility that there might be a war somewhere . . . none of this bothered me, because I was married, I had a new husband, I thought I was getting out of the Army in another year. And it really didn't hit me that he might go to Vietnam. I mean that never really dawned on me until early '65. We had this one patient who'd been in special forces and he was a quadraplegic when we got him. He was unable to move anything. He was in a coma, and we had him for several months. He had been ambushed. He was an adviser and he had been ambushed by the Viet Cong. When he came out of this coma, which he was in for a couple of months, he began to talk to us about some of the things that were happening. He told us this wasn't going to be just advisers. This was going to be big and it was already getting bigger. And that was when it dawned on me that there's something going on.

But I guess I didn't really think it was going to affect us. I really didn't. My husband had been stationed at Fort Sam for quite awhile, I guess maybe five years at that time. So he was well overdue to go somewhere. But he thought he was going to have a long tour, which means Germany or Japan. This was early 1965. By that time I was assistant head nurse on the neurosurgical floor. Then in May of '65 we went on leave, and his orders were waiting for him when we got back. They were for Vietnam. They were alert orders at that time, which just simply meant that you're going, we don't know when, but at some point in time you're going to Vietnam.

They assigned him to the 498th Air Ambulance Company, a unit they were pulling together from all over. So he was on alert until he got his final orders. We had managed to go home in June and he got his orders after we got back. He left in late July. I believe he left in July because we had gone home—yeah, that's what it was—we had gone home the whole month of June. I didn't believe it was going to happen. He wasn't going to go anywhere. We went to the Farmer's Daughter the week before he left, and George Jones was playing there that night. He was my husband's favorite country singer and he played "Walk Through this World" for us because my husband was going to Vietnam. So while we were dancing, I could think, "It's all a big joke, he's not going." But he did. And he went very quickly. In January we'd never heard of Vietnam and now here it was July and he gets a call early on a Sunday morning saying, "It's on, we're going." He had been on alert, which meant his bags were packed. We had to get him off to the airport quickly, where they issued him a weapon. I kissed him good-bye and he was gone. I didn't know where he was going immediately, and he didn't know either. They flew him out on a military plane from San Antonio airport. Later, I found out they went to Oakland and left on a ship. But I didn't know a thing until he called me from San Francisco. So I knew he was leaving by ship. But he wasn't able to tell me precisely where they were going. We all assumed it was Vietnam, but they were not told specifically.

Imagine them issuing him a rifle in San Antonio airport! That's when it really struck me, "My God, he could get killed over there." You know, they're going to be shooting at people. So for the next month I heard nothing. There were several things going through my mind. First of all, I wasn't sure if I was pregnant. That was number one. The second thing was that I would be getting out of the military fairly soon. I could've gotten out in January of '66, because that would have completed my two-year tour. That had been the plan. I was going to get out and wait for him to come back. But my thoughts were just simply that I was afraid. I was afraid for him. We'd only been married nine months.

He left on a Sunday morning. I cried all night, but Monday I had to go to work, I was on duty. I didn't hear from him, there was no communication. Finally, in September, I heard something. He had arrived in Vietnam. They had gone in to Qui Nhon. And the first night there his unit had been under attack. The very first night. In the first letter that I got from him, he said that they were attached to the 8th Field Hospital and they were going to be stationed in Nha Trang. It was a hospital, and did I want to go? He asked me, "Do you want to come to Vietnam? Ask for orders." Well, in the meantime I found out I was not pregnant, OK, so that was not a problem. So, did I want to go to Vietnam? Are you kidding me, of course I did! My husband was there! I had no conception of what Vietnam was. I just wanted to be with my husband. So I forgot about getting out of the Army. There was a hospital over there, and my husband needed me. I was Miss Nightingale, ready to go. I asked for orders immediately . . . the next day. I mean I couldn't wait to get to the hospital to ask for orders. And I was told right away, you're not needed. We don't need any nurses in Vietnam. Well, that was the September 1965 buildup and I think something like 100,000 men were going over. And they were telling me that they didn't need any nurses? That was crazy! I was a fairly hot-headed young lady at the time. I still have that problem to some extent, but I've learned to control it a little bit. But I decided it was against God and everything else to keep a man and wife separated. And if there was any way possible, I was going to go. I argued with the chief nurse, and I cried, and I fussed, and she said, "No way, you're not going."

So I decided I'm going to talk to this friend of mine who had a friend who had a friend—you know that kind of deal. So I did, and he said, "Well, it's a possibility, let me get back to you." So I waited. In the meantime the chief nurse called me and said I was going to be on alert orders to Okinawa. And I said, "I don't want to go to Okinawa. That's not close enough. I want to go to Vietnam." She said, "Well, sorry about that. You're going to Okinawa, you're on alert orders and you're going to Okinawa." I said, "Well, then you can send me to Okinawa for the next four or five months, but then you're going to have to let me out because you can't extend me. My time is up, and I won't extend." Anyway, I went crying to this person again, this friend. And he said how long do you have. I said, "Well, she says the orders are going to be in next week." The alert orders. And once I get those I'm stuck. He said, "Well, let me see if I can't get you alert orders for Vietnam before you get alert orders for Okinawa." He was just an officer who was a friend who had a friend. But he had friends in Washington. And he called his friends in Washington and got me what I wanted. And so, by Monday morning I was on alert orders to the 8th Field Hospital in Nha Trang. It was amazing! The chief nurse was not happy. I had 10 days to get myself all together and finish up everything in San Antonio. That's what I was told. It wasn't until November that I actually got travel orders. And I was given 30 days leave, also. So all of December I was home. My actual orders to leave for Vietnam were set for the 3rd of January, 1966, my birthday.

I arrived in Vietnam two days later. Actually we had skipped a day in between, because you lose that day going to Vietnam. I landed January 5th, 1966. I was the only woman on board the plane to begin with. There was me and 50–55 guys, and, I was treated royally. But actually, I ended up playing stewardess on that flight for the men. I'm from an older traditional family, and you feel like—when you're a woman and there's men all around that's sort of what you end up doing, at least at that time. But I will say this much, they stood guard when I used the only restroom on the plane.

I arrived at Tan Son Nhut at five in the morning and it was dark. And I got off the plane and this little guy comes running up to me, a private, saying, "Are you MACV personnel?" I didn't even know what MACV personnel was. And I said I don't think so. He said, "Well, you're a woman, come with me." I thought, "Oh no, what am I getting into." Anyway, we went to this jeep and he said, "Don't worry about anything. If any shooting starts, just duck down in the jeep." I can remember thinking, "I just want to go back to my mother. I want back on the plane. I don't really want to see my husband. I just want to go home." And indeed there were tracers flying every now and again, and it was just like a dream. Almost like a dream, and I was going to wake up and I wouldn't be there.

And so he takes me into Camp Alpha, sort of a temporary camp with nothing but tents and men. All of a sudden a cry goes up, "Round eye in the camp." What is a round eye? You have to realize that early on in the war when we went to Vietnam we weren't told anything about Vietnam. There were no indoctrination or training sessions or anything else. There was nothing. You were just told you were going to Vietnam and it was some country that was somewhere in Southeast Asia. But you didn't know anything about it. So I had no idea what he meant by "round eye." But all of a sudden here are men in various stages of undress all over the camp, paying attention to me. It made you feel pretty good, I'll say that, but it was kind of like "what's going on here?"

It became clear that if I was going to get to Nha Trang, I was going to have to hitch a ride. So I went back to Tan Son Nhut so I could check with the various companies that were sending planes out and see if anybody was going to Nha Trang. And by company, I don't mean like airline companies. I checked around, going from place to place. "Are you sending a plane to Nha Trang today?" And the answer was always, "No, we're not going there today." Finally this one guy said yes, he was taking a plane out to Nha Trang, but I couldn't go. "Why not?" "Because we don't have a bathroom on the plane." "I'll hold it for the two hours or whatever I'm going to be on the plane." Finally, after I used a few tears, he said, "OK, you can ride on the plane. We'll take you in to Nha Trang." So I gathered up my duffel bag and everything and got on the plane.

I got to Nha Trang and my husband wasn't there. And I mean I panicked because I didn't . . . you know, he was supposed to meet me at the plane. So I'm standing there with my duffel bag, 'cause the plane had taxied off and everybody else was gone, and now I'm standing there in the rain, what do I do? Anyway, my husband had been waiting, but he had become so discouraged because I hadn't come in that he left. And this friend of his said, "Look she said she was coming in today, she's coming in today. I'm going to wait." So, lucky for me, somebody had waited, because he came and picked me up and took me to my husband. To the best of my knowledge we were the first married couple stationed in Vietnam. For this reason they had no quarters for us. So we didn't go on base. In fact, he had rented something that was basically a motel room.

The whole plane ride over I was really frightened because we'd only been married nine months when he left. And I kept thinking, "I don't know who he is. I don't know him. And I'm not going to recognize him and I probably don't even love him anymore, because I don't know him." I was really scared about that. And very frightened that he wouldn't care about me anymore; that, you know, I was flying off to this godforsaken place, and I'd be stuck there with a man I didn't know and didn't love. And there's a war going on and I might get shot at. But he did recognize me. We had a nice evening and he took me downtown the first evening. We went out to dinner. And at that time, versus later in the war, Nha Trang was probably the second, third largest city in Vietnam. It was a resort. The French had used it as a place for vacation. And there were these beautiful, beautiful villas built on the beach.

I was assigned to the medical side of the 8th Field Hospital. We had a 36-bed unit, somewhat like an intensive care unit today. It was a building that was actually air conditioned, which was unbelievable. However, most of the time the air conditioning didn't work, so that was a problem. Most of the patients were recovering from malaria, dengue fever, and various other tropical diseases. Also we had guys in there with things like heart attacks, psychosis, drug overdoses, and alcoholism. We were also responsible for the preoperative unit, which was where all the casualties came into. Initially they would go to the emergency room and then come to us for pre-oping. Then they'd go to surgery and then to the post-operative side. We also had an isolation tent outside that was used for some of the respiratory diseases. That was like a 20-bed tent. So if you add it all up, you come up with a lot of patients. The only females were the RNs. There were no female doctors in our unit. There were no female corpsmen or LVNs. None at all. And there were no female anything else either, except for the Red Cross workers. They were the only other females. But one nurse was responsible for those areas. And the unit was not very big at that time. We had maybe 20 women, total.

I remember being told we were getting a hundred patients in. Now that was medical and pre-operative. We had no beds. So we had to air evac out a hundred patients so we would have beds for the ones coming in. Now I was not alone at that time, because the thing that was neat about Vietnam was that you really did work together. Yes, there was one nurse assigned to a shift. Not day shift—day shift had more. On the 3-to-11 and 11-to-7 shifts there was one RN assigned. But the nice thing was that you knew you could call for help if you needed it. So if you got a mass-cal coming in, you could call and you'd get help. If I were 3-to-11 and I knew a mass-cal was coming in at 11, I wouldn't go back to my villa. I would stay there and work through the night with whoever was on. Or we'd call day shift to come in early. So you always had people you could call on and there were times that we worked 24 to 36 hours straight.

During one of these ordeals, we got in a Korean with a live round in his head. That was bad. The Koreans were also stationed in Vietnam. The White Horse Division was stationed in Nha Trang, and this particular Korean had been shot in the head and was alive when he got to the hospital. And we were examining him and all I can remember is that somebody looked into his eye and said, "Oh my God, there's a live round in here." He had an unexploded shell, a mortar shell, in his head and it was sticking out the one eye. So they X-rayed him quickly. And indeed, there was a shell sitting right there. And it was unexploded, which means it's live. It could've gone off any time. Well in the meantime, he died. So now what do you do with a dead body that has a live round in it? Nobody knew what to do. The Koreans didn't want him back. The morgue was right next to the medical unit where I worked. So we sandbagged the morgue, and we put the body in there until someone could decide what to do. The choices were real simple. One of the docs could go in and try to remove it, but we didn't have enough doctors to begin with. And if he went in and it went off, we could very easily lose a doctor. And this was not a live patient. They could set it off somehow. Or they could give him back to the Koreans. Well, the Koreans didn't want him. The final upshot was that they set it off.

We had another guy who had been sprayed with a machine gun just up and down. I can still see the patterns of the bullet holes just up and down. He made it, by the way. They came in planes, ambulances, helicopters . . . I mean I just remember that as a blur of noises and patients being brought in. The medical patients—these guys didn't want to be sick. If you were sick that meant you were taking away from somebody else, and your unit might get ambushed, and you wouldn't be there. So they'd wait until they were so sick that their temperatures were up to 106 degrees. These guys were so dehydrated—they'd been puking for days and having diarrhea. I've never seen such sick people as I saw in Vietnam. We'd get in people with punji stick wounds. The sticks were smeared with all kinds of junk, and these guys would come in after stepping on them.

We had one guy who sticks out in my mind. He was with the 101st Airborne, or it might have been 1st Cav. And anyway, we'd gotten an ambushed unit in. And this was . . . I had been in Vietnam a couple of weeks, a month maybe, I don't even remember anymore. But we'd gotten this ambushed unit in, and this guy said his unit had been ambushed and the Viet Cong had captured the two medics from the unit. And they had skinned them alive, cut off their testicles, put them in their mouths, and hung the two medics in the trail. And he told, he told me this, you know that the . . . he couldn't believe, I mean he just couldn't believe that one human being would do that to somebody else. And they did that to two of our medics. And medics were very valuable people in Vietnam. The units really protected their medics. And for something like that to be done to two of them . . . and of course then they were waiting in ambush when the unit came upon them. And one of them was not dead yet. We never got him though. He died, he was dead. To see that. This guy couldn't have been more than 19 or 20 himself. You know, to me that was . . . I thought, "How could they, how could anything we do be wrong?" It was sort of like you've got to fight fire with fire. And I've never been able to understand since then why anything we did is wrong. I mean war is wrong. OK, but there's no good way to fight a war. There's no . . . it's a no-win situation no matter what you do, because people are going to die. And to me, you know, it seems more humane to just shoot somebody than to do those kinds of things. That was the worst, the very worst that I had heard or saw.

At the time, I never really questioned the war. My country said go, and I went. I really was patriotic . . . in spite of the fact that my husband was there and I wanted to see him! My father had been a medic in World War II in the South Pacific, and I had grown up loving the flag, the whole bit. I'd been a Girl Scout. I joined the Army for more than just a broken love affair, for God's sake! I did really want to be a military nurse. I had no concept of what war was, though. And when my husband went to Vietnam, I really wanted to go for him, to be there for him. But I also had a Florence Nightingale streak in me. When I got to Vietnam, I still didn't know what war was. But when that unit was ambushed, I knew what it was then. I really felt like we were here for a purpose and we're going to do it. We're going to win. We have to. And I guess I felt that way pretty much throughout my tour. Toward the end of my tour, which would have been the last part of '66, it seemed like there were some stories that some of the men weren't allowed to do this and they weren't allowed to do that, and why didn't we let them fight the war the way war should be fought. But that was just real kind of nebulous stuff. I guess it was in the next couple of years that we really began to say, "What's going on over here? How much longer?" But at that time, things were very patriotic still. And there wasn't that big anti-Vietnam mood in the states yet.

I was lucky. I had both the physical and emotional support of my husband. So, in that way, I was different than anyone else who was serving. I spent time talking with the other nurses, too, don't get me wrong. I didn't just run home to my husband. I mean we were together a lot, the other nurses and I, but they didn't have that kind of close person they could go to. They developed close relationships of their own. But I don't think it's quite the same thing. I knew that I could count on his emotional support. I could tell him things that you really have to get out. In nursing, whether it's in Vietnam or anywhere else, when you have stressful things that you have to deal with, you'll explode if you keep them inside long enough. And there was a lot inside me.

The worst casualty, except maybe for the Korean . . . the worst one that sticks out in my mind was just before I went home. And that was the guy who was hit by a flame thrower, full face, full front. And he was an older American. Older at that time was like in his late 20s or early 30s. It was just around Christmas time, and he'd been hit full face with the flame thrower. And we had saved him. I was not there when he came in. I took care of him the next day. So I don't know how he came in. But I can remember I was going home and he wasn't. And that thought has stuck in my mind for years. He had a picture of three kids in his wallet. And he couldn't speak. He had a trach. We had a bird ventilator at that time . . . this was before the breathing machines were really big, big items. We had one in our hospital. So that's how he was surviving, and I kept thinking, "You know, why are they doing this? Why are they prolonging this man's agony, because he's not going to live?" There was no way this guy was going to live. He was burned too badly. His face, his whole front . . . he was burned to a crisp. There was no way this man was going to live. His face wasn't bandaged. It was open and it was . . . he didn't have a face. There was a hole for his trach, and a hole where the mouth should be, and he didn't have . . . all you could hear was the breathing machine going. He wasn't going home. He wasn't going home. And I kept thinking, I'm going home and he's not. At that point I was on my alert to go home. I was going home, he wasn't. And he had three kids waiting.

To this day I will never know how my husband and I managed to spend our entire tour together. One thing I neglected to mention was that about three weeks after I arrived in Nha Trang, the chief nurse in Vietnam came through and she saw me and she said, "What are you doing here?" I said I was told to come on to Nha Trang. And she said, "Who told you that?" I said they had called for me and that . . . well, as it turned out she didn't even know that I was in Vietnam. She could have pulled me out at that time and sent me to another hospital. But I guess somebody was watching over me, because she didn't. She left me there.

We couldn't live on post; so what we did, we got a villa downtown. The 8th Field Hospital was on an air base. And that air base in Nha Trang was very heavily guarded. It had an air strip long enough to accommodate jets. And the town was right there, up close to the base. We couldn't live on base because we didn't have housing. So we got this little villa. It was a beautiful little villa in downtown, and my husband had a motor bike and we rode back and forth as though we were holding normal, civilian-type jobs. We lived there for three months, I mean it was like we were on a vacation or something. If there hadn't been a war going on, we never would have known. This was still early on in the war. But even so, after about three months, Nha Trang wasn't sacred any more. There was some fighting going on, and there was a lot of student unrest in the town. And so the military told us we had to move. Either we had to come back on post—he would have to live with his unit and I would have to live with mine—or we would have to find someplace that was safe where we could live. Well, right across from the 50-caliber machine guns that guarded the entrance to the base and the hospital there was a little row of two-room shacks. They were not great, but we moved in there.

There was a down side to my personal life in Vietnam. My husband and I have had a lot of problems, and much of it started in Vietnam. He drank a lot, so there were a lot of bad times in Vietnam with him there; but they were overshadowed, I think, by the good times—the support he gave me. There were times I was worried for him. One of the nights when we had a red alert, which means we were under attack, I didn't know where he was. And until I knew where he was, I was non-functional. I was no help at all. The Viet Cong were attacking the base. There was a tent city a mile from the hospital. It was a huge base for personnel and they had blown up the mess hall, so we had gotten a lot of casualties in. The VC were actually attacking the hospital at that point. They were heading for us, and there was a lot of shooting going on. And until I knew where he was, I couldn't function. I could not function. So that's a bad side of having your husband with you. And I'm sure from what he said that the same was true of him. He was so worried about me that it was hard for him to be able to function.

I feel like our personal life suffered because of the effects of alcohol. I didn't drink much, but he did. Vietnam didn't inspire his drinking, but it sure augmented it. He drank before we went to Vietnam. But he could keep it pretty much under control. There was no control in Vietnam. He would drink, not all the time, but when he did it was a good one. We've had a lot of lasting problems with that. He's a recovered alcoholic now, and I'm very proud of him for that. He's been recovered for 10 years. But it took a big toll, a big toll on our lives. Alcohol caused a lot of physical and verbal abuse on both sides. And finally I said, "I'm not going to take any more of this," and that is when he finally got some help. Vietnam did that. Vietnam is where he really started drinking heavily. As I say, the drinking didn't start there, but the heavy drinking did. And Vietnam was a year of heavy drinking. But we went through so much together in Vietnam that I felt like no matter what, I couldn't leave him.

The only time I ever got any flack about my husband was once when he was injured in a fight. He ended up going over our balcony and landed on his arms, and so he really was injured. Of course, he had been drinking. The surgical side saw him first. They really didn't care too much about seeing what was wrong with him. So I had him admitted to medicine. But that was the only time when they told me: you know you're supposed to be on duty, not worrying about your husband. It wasn't a particularly busy time. I can remember times when we were busy, though, where people with alcoholic problems would just sort of be set aside. What could you do? And at that point no one thought my husband was an alcoholic. He just drank. We all drank. I drank, too. But not to the extent that I couldn't work. Nobody ever showed up on duty drunk that I ever remember. You just didn't do that, because you had a job to do. My husband never showed up drunk on duty, either. He just didn't do that.

When you're together in a situation where you could be dead soon, it's like you live every minute to the fullest. We lived. We had so many experiences outside of the hospital situation, both good and bad. We really lived in Vietnam when we were off duty. Everybody did. Oh yeah, there was gambling, partying, drinking, eating, loving. You did a lot, because you didn't know how long you had. You never knew when the next mass-cal was going to come in, which meant you might be working hours and hours and hours; or you didn't know when you were going to be attacked. So therefore, you lived life to the fullest. The fights that would occur in Vietnam between us over his drinking were terrible, but the making up was fantastic. We were so close together. And I'm certain that closeness made it impossible to leave him. I don't know if that makes sense. A lot of women wouldn't take the kinds of things I have, but if you're in the states it's a lot easier to leave. You can go home to mom or whatever. When you're all alone in a foreign country and there's fighting going on, it's awfully hard. And I think that pulled us together. The commitment to each other, the fact that we had gone through Vietnam together . . . well, it was as though after going through that, we could lick anything.

We both had our orders to come home together. We got to Saigon and there was some confusion over where we were going to be processed out. But once we got that straight, we were back at Tan Son Nhut. They went through this thing of saying your name, your flight is scheduled out day after tomorrow, and so on. This would have been on the 30th of December at eleven o'clock in the morning. We were to come back at least two hours ahead of time. So I told my husband, we better make sure we're back early. So we spent the next night in Saigon. We found a hotel room, spent the night in Saigon. And we went back to Tan Son Nhut early . . . just in case. We got there and found out that our names weren't on the manifest to fly home, which means you don't go. Once again, womanly wiles worked. I cried my way into a seat on the plane. And then I equally cried *his* way on, because I said I wasn't leaving anywhere without him.

The first thing we did when we got home was go on 30 days leave to Pennsylvania and then to Louisiana to visit my husband's family. And then we were both stationed back at Fort Sam Houston, right back to San Antonio. Same place where we started—the Beach Pavilion. It was funny arriving in San Francisco. It was like nobody cared, I mean like nobody bothered. They weren't angry with us either, I heard that happened later on. It was like nothing—"Oh, so you've been to Vietnam, what's that?" It was like nobody really cared. At that time, I don't think we really wanted to talk about it either. It was like you were just two days out of Vietnam and you really just wanted to relax, to be clean, warm, have good food, a drink—the whole bit. But my parents were real good. They asked a lot of questions, they listened. We talked a lot about Vietnam. They were just real open. My friends, that was another story. They didn't really want to hear about anything. And his family didn't really understand. His family was very old fashioned, and they just didn't understand any of it.

When I got to Fort Sam, I found none of the nurses wanted to hear about Vietnam either. It was so early in the war that very few people had been there. Nobody wanted to hear about it. It wasn't that they were hostile. I can remember one night we were called and told we were getting five patients in, five admissions. And I said, "Oh, that's nothing, you know I can handle that. In Vietnam we had a hundred patients at a time coming in." And I'd get, "Oh well, that's nice." Nobody cared. Nobody really cared. It was an anticlimax, because by that time I was ready to talk about it. I wanted people to listen, and they wouldn't. You have all these experiences because, in spite of everything, Vietnam was the ultimate in nursing experiences. It taught me that I was a good nurse, that I could function with minimum equipment under maximum stress. We had to improvise equipment. Chest tube drainage would have to be done with old bottles. Half the time you didn't have the supplies you needed. My husband and I rode to Cam Ranh Bay to pick up juice for patients, because you had water that you couldn't drink. I mean it was awful. Did you ever try to drink chlorinated water? It's terrible. And so the patients needed something to drink, but they'd get sick on that water. So we rode to Cam Ranh Bay. He was up in the mess hall, so he knew that a shipment of juice had come in. And although it was illegal for us to do that—I was AWOL essentially—we went. We wanted to tell people about this stuff, and nobody wanted to listen.

We were getting a good number of casualties from Vietnam by the time I got to the Beach Pavilion. It was almost as though they trailed me home. I finally wound up on the orthopedic ward, which took up the entire third floor with one unit having nothing but amputations. The war definitely wasn't over for me. We had a lot who had three, four limbs gone. We had one who had three limbs gone and was blind. For what? That's when the waste really hit you. That's when it really hit you, because it's not like you're immediately taking care of them now, like you're saving their life. Now you had time to think about what the hell you saved them for. You know, what good is it? And that was bad, that was really bad. There were so many young men who lost everything . . . lost their legs, their genitals. We had one who had a hemipelvectomy on both sides, which means his legs were blown off all the way. I mean there was nothing from the navel down.

I tried talking to some of them. I can remember them trying to respond when I said I was in Vietnam, too. And there were happy times, too. I remember the wheel chair races in the hall. And the competitions. You had to really be hard, though, you had to be hard because if you weren't hard they could sit there and just wallow in self-pity. There were a couple, though, like the guy who had everything blown off and the one who was blind and had three limbs blown off, that you just really hoped would die. You really hoped they would. I don't know if the blind one did though. We lost so many. Losing the genitals, that was absolutely the worst. For them it was like life isn't worth living anymore . . . there's nothing they can do. They can't get married. They can't satisfy a woman, they can't. . . . They aren't even a man anymore. So what good are they? This is the kind of thing they were thinking. That was stressful work. Most of the time, I just really wanted to cry. I was in Vietnam early. The casualties weren't as bad as they were later on. I mean we didn't have Agent Orange. We didn't have as many young men compared to what came later. We had a lot of seasoned troops over there early on. There were men who had been in the military for a long time. In a way, Vietnam didn't make the impression on me that coming home to the Beach Pavilion did. In 1967 there were . . . I don't even know how many amputees we saw through that place. It was like it was never ending. They kept coming. And there were so many and they were all so young. And there were more coming in all the time.

I think the best thing Vietnam did was to show me what nursing is and can be. But after that high, there came the inevitable low. I came back just really dissatisfied with nursing. Back in the states, you weren't allowed to do anything. It was like all of a sudden your judgment wasn't trusted, you didn't have any smarts. You had to ask the physician for permission to do everything. And it wasn't that way in Vietnam. You worked together with the physicians and others as a team. And we all knew our jobs. And we all performed them well. That was in Vietnam. Suddenly you come back to the states and it's not that way. Of course, it wasn't that bad in the military hospitals. There weren't enough physicians and there were certainly a lot of patients. So you had to take on added responsibilities, because there just weren't enough physicians. I got out of the military in 1968 and went to Germany to join my husband. And I got a job as a civilian in a military hospital. I was in a supervisory position in Germany, so it was somewhat different for me there, too.

I came back to the states as a civilian, working as a nursing director in a nursing home. There you couldn't do anything without having a doctor sign for it. And I had all these ideas and thoughts and just couldn't, couldn't do a thing, because you had to have physician backup. And that's when I started thinking there's got to be more. There's got to be a way to get more out of civilian nursing, because I'm not happy this way. And so I went back to school. And I'd been out 12 years at that point. I became a pediatric nurse practitioner. I had started working with children in Germany and then continued that for three years in the states prior to going to school. But I did go back, and I got my bachelor's degree; but I still wasn't satisfied. So I decided I wanted more. That's why I got a master's degree and started teaching. I'm very active in professional organizations.

I think all of that stems from this need to be the best I can, do the best I can, and that started in Vietnam. I think some of it was there before, don't get me wrong. I don't think that suddenly, magically, I was endowed with something in Vietnam. But Vietnam showed me what you can do . . . what can be done as a nurse. It was the best nursing experience I'll ever have, particularly in terms of psychological care, because you had to listen to people. You did. Now I buried a lot of that. But I'm still a good listener, and I can get people to listen to me. Just the other day at the hospital, we had a very traumatic case with a child who had lost his father and sister. And the mother was sitting there, she looked like she needed to talk. So I spent half an hour getting her to ventilate about what was going on in her life, about losing her husband and child, and having the other child injured. It's that kind of thing that I learned in Vietnam. It may have been there all along, but Vietnam brought it out. For me, Vietnam was the thing that showed me the way I wanted to go, the kind of nurse I wanted to be.

Also, if it weren't for Vietnam, I think my husband and I would not be together. We had only each other in Vietnam, there's something about that. I come from a family that says you work on your marriage, which probably helped. I don't think we would have survived without a situation that required that kind of closeness. I've seen too many others break up because the bond wasn't that strong. We still have our problems. Everybody does. But we've made it to our twenty-first wedding anniversary. I think the worst times are over. We had three years of psychotherapy after Vietnam for his drinking and the problems that we were having. We've gone through individual and joint therapy. And I think that that helped me to understand myself a whole lot better. All the talking that you do in psychotherapy makes you stop and look at yourself and think about what really matters to you, what things are really important. I discovered I was important to myself. That's probably the main thing. But I also discovered that I really cared about him. There had been a lot of times when I thought that maybe I didn't. You know, there was a period of about five, six years between Vietnam and the time we actually got help. And in that time period there were many, many times that I thought I couldn't take anymore, but I always did. In the psychotherapeutic sessions over those three years, I think we both learned that we're important individually and that we have to work very hard together. It doesn't just happen. That was something I hadn't thought about, that we really both had to contribute a lot to the marriage. In a sense, Vietnam created our problem, but it also ensured our survival. I don't know what else could have done it. That was the one year where all we had was each other. We really had each other.

Laura Radnor

I met Bernard halfway through my tour. I knew my way around
pretty well by the time he arrived. He was just a friendly
guy—a friendly guy who kept pursuing me, you know, coming
around and talking. And for a long time, it was just like we found
ourselves not on duty, so it was time to talk. We just became very
good friends. He was a doctor, a surgeon. I thought we were about
the same age, but later on I found out he lied to me. He was really
three years younger and he was afraid to tell me. I think he didn't
look on himself as being mature or something along that line. But I
knew he was married and after awhile he told me that he and his
wife were separated. They had separated before he came over. I'm
not real comfortable talking about this.

There were a lot of lesbians there, which I wasn't. I'd never been
around lesbians before in my life. I didn't know anything about it.
But most of them worked where I worked in the intensive care unit.
And they were very interesting people and I enjoyed talking with
them. Well, this was one of the things that when Bernard and I first
started talking together, I guess it intrigued him. Either that or he
teased me about it, I don't know which. I guess he teased me about
whether I was a lesbian or not. I teased him back by not answering
directly. You know, "Whatever you believe, just believe it." I think

*Laura Radnor is a pseudonym for a nurse who served in Vietnam in
1967–1968, and who now lives in San Antonio. Certain names, places and
other details have been changed throughout the text.*

that was the impression I gave him. I'm not one prone to deny things. You know, if someone wants to say something about me, well, that's fine with me. Do whatever you want. I try to live the best I can. I try to be as forthright as I know how, and whatever you think, well, that's your problem.

I guess I probably intrigued him. I certainly don't know what he saw in me, other than that I was a woman, an American woman, in a place where the odds pretty much were against him. We were totally different. He was raised in a family with money, about as totally different as you can get from my background. He was from Chicago, and I was from rural Louisiana. Just totally different backgrounds. But it seems . . . it was so funny. I pointed this out to him. We've discussed this several times, the difference in our backgrounds. He's Jewish and I'm Baptist. But still we had a lot to talk about. As a matter of fact, one of our favorite topics for discussion was our different backgrounds and the ways we were raised.

Physicians were being drafted at the time. It was a two-year commitment. Of course, one year was Vietnam. His feelings about Vietnam were pretty much the same as mine. He probably didn't feel like I felt before he came over, because this was something he had to do. He was drafted; I volunteered. There weren't a lot of people like myself who volunteered, especially among the physicians.

I look back on it today and I have trouble pinpointing what it was I found attractive in him. There were hundreds of guys there, and often I ask myself "why was it that one?" I think it's because we . . . because he just liked to talk to me. He was a skillful conversationalist, and he wasn't too obvious about putting the "make" on me. I liked to talk to him, and I found myself looking forward to the times when he'd come around my ward. I guess he just found in me a friend that he needed. And I found in him a friend that I needed. And we're still very good friends.

Eventually, we became lovers, but it wasn't right away. I really don't remember how we got there after being just "friends." It was a subtle change; it just happened one day. I don't know why I needed him so much. Why does anybody need anybody? The war had something to do with it, needless to say. I mean, this was a different kind of a relationship from what I would have gotten into if I'd stayed in New Orleans, or been assigned to a stateside Army hospital. Here we were in a foreign land involved in a situation that left a lot of us wondering. We spent a lot of time together wondering would we ever get back home. That was always in your mind, would we ever get out of here? Being confined to the hospital compound, not being able to get off the compound at night, or not being able to do a lot of things . . . that was hard. We pretty much had to rely on ourselves. There was no place to go and nothing to do, so you always met outside your hooches and you'd sit in the quadrangle and you'd watch the stars. And everybody was there together, there with maybe popcorn; or maybe it wouldn't be everybody, it would be just one or two people and everything would come out because there was time for you to talk about everything, and you talked about everything from the time when you were small till you were old, and what you were going to do when you went home.

We sang a lot. Anyone who could play the guitar was always welcome. We sang "100 miles," no, it was "500 miles." We sang "Mickey Mouse." We had a refrigeration ship that sat in our harbor because we were on the coast. And on Sundays we could get on one of these Navy boats and go out there and the crew was so nice, they were happy to see the whole group and they would grill steaks usually. Of course they had all the booze there was in the world. That was a Sunday excursion if you were off on Sunday.

I was there a year and I don't think I went to the leprosarium, for instance, more than three times at the most and went on medcaps maybe twice. I went on one medcap with Bernard. With us, mostly it was going to the club and eating and just sharing time . . . off duty time. I would go by the OR where he worked, when it was not too busy. It was just a lot of time sharing. After awhile, it didn't matter what we were doing as long as we were together. The more time I spent with him, the more time I needed with him.

I was born in Louisiana. We moved around some in the 1930s, but we eventually came back to Louisiana when I was in elementary school. My parents separated, so we lived out in the country near my mother's people. We were very poor when we grew up. We had plenty of food, but we were poor in this world's goods. And my mother's favorite first cousin went to nursing school. Probably she was a role model for me. Other than that, I don't know what possessed me to even want to do anything, because nobody in that part of the country went on to school. They usually got married. And I decided I wanted to be an English teacher or a nurse. And of course, going to college was out of the question.

I always felt like I was different. Everyone else always seemed to have more than I did. And probably they didn't. You know nobody really had very much, and I just wanted more and wanted to get out of there. I moved to New Orleans in 1961. I worked in a hospital and I dated a guy there, and that didn't work out. It was 1967 and I felt like I needed a career change. But I was still a diploma graduate, so my prospects for promotion were not great. So I started looking around for other things to do. And I thought about the public health system. I just wanted to go somewhere and do something different. In the meantime I was going to college at night for a few quarters, and I just wasn't getting anywhere fast. And then one day I saw an ad on TV about wanting nurses in Vietnam. And I had had some pretty strong feelings about the war there. I was a Goldwater supporter, or at least I had been. And I had a pretty strong feeling and I thought, "Go to Vietnam." This just hit me one day—"Go to Vietnam." So I called the Army recruiter and I said, "Do you send nurses to Vietnam?" The guy seemed a little shocked and he said, "Yes, do you have 10 friends who want to go with you?" I said, "No, just me." So they did up my paperwork with guaranteed assignment to Vietnam. That was in September of '67. I was commissioned in October and went to basic at Fort Sam Houston on November 5th.

Basic training was a new world for me. It was meeting a lot of people, which I enjoyed, and having to scurry around. Things were very busy; they didn't have housing available on the post, so we had to find an apartment off post that would house us for six weeks. I lived over on Mulberry Street. And it was really exciting. These were fast times, fast moving, everything focused on Vietnam. I guess that may have heightened the anticipation and everything. As part of our orientation we had courses in wound care, suturing, and doing cricoidotomies on goats. And see, my nursing experience up to this time had been very benign as far as trauma was concerned. I hadn't seen or cared for hardly any, just the elective surgery type of stuff is all I had ever taken care of.

Our training group was really big. We had other people in it be-

sides nurses. I think there were about 200 people or so. I was a
platoon leader too, because I was older. You know, here I am 10
years out of nursing school and because I was just a diploma graduate, I could only come in as a first lieutenant. But still I was 32,
which was the limit, so I guess people looked to me as a leader. I
usually fit in quite well with younger people. I enjoyed being a platoon leader even though I was lacking very greatly in confidence. I
had to call cadence when we were marching. I had to call formation
and put our group together. I had squad leaders and we were constantly checking the roster . . . "squad so-and-so—all present, sir,"
that kind of thing. We practiced marching everyday at noon, and
sometimes the band would come out. This was at old Medical Field
Service School, before the Academy of Health Sciences that's now
in existence. We drilled on what we called the quadrangle sur-
rounded on four sides by barracks and other buildings. Today, it's a
big parking lot. We had to have about an hour of marching everyday.
And it was fun. I wasn't the best platoon leader in the world, I'm
sure. One day I actually marched my group into a wall! But I tell
you, when we left they gave me a gift. The platoon gave me a cam-
era. I was really touched by that.

About two weeks before we got out of basic they called—it was
about 13 of us—they called us out and told us we were going directly to Vietnam. I was really stunned. I thought, "I've asked for
this and now it's here. How will I handle it?" Imagine going straight
to Vietnam from basic. And a lot of the nurses had no experience.
They were right out of school.

My attitude toward the war at that time was that we need to get in
there, end it, and get out. Of course, we were going over there to
fight communists. I really felt strongly hawkish. I felt like it was just
lingering too long and we needed to get in and win the war and get
out. The prospect of going to Vietnam was exciting. My impression
after I came to basic was that we probably would live in tents, probably wouldn't have any hot water, running water, and of course the
latrines, you know, all that good stuff. I was ready for a change. I
needed a change. You read about the protests against the war in the
papers, but I don't remember seeing any of it. And of course it was
obvious to me that Johnson was doing everything that Goldwater
said he was going to do, and now everybody was protesting against

it. For myself, you know, I didn't feel like I could end the war. All I could do was just help. Help our people. But the thing was, I got there and I hadn't been there a month and I totally changed my mind.

Upon our arrival in Saigon, I had the feeling that they didn't quite know what to do with all these females. Finally, they got a bus with all these bars around it and then they got a jeep with a machine gun mounted on it—two jeeps, one in the front and one in the back—and they bused us to the replacement center at Long Binh. So we got out there and it was like one or two o'clock in the morning. They issued sheets to us, and sent us out to these little hooches that were just as dusty or dirty as they could be, and we had to bathe in cold water. Now talk about primitive, that place was primitive. The next day, though, we got to see the chief nurse. She welcomed us to Vietnam, and started making assignments.

Just before I left to go to my unit, I went in the PX and bought one of those Australian bush hats. Not being familiar with the military dress code, I thought it was legal to wear them. After all, they were green. So I arrived at my new hospital in a brand new, jaunty Australian bush hat. Of course, I was promptly told to remove it. And that was my greeting to the hospital. Oh dear, I think of some of the things that went on and it's crazy. I knew the war was everywhere. No place was sacred as far as lines were concerned. I think I was aware of that. There were no amenities whatsoever. We lived in these hooches, formed around a quadrangle in the middle, and we spent a lot of time out there sun bathing or playing basketball or volleyball. The whole bit.

Our first duty on arriving was to work a few days on the POW ward. It was required. I went in and I thought to myself, "This is the enemy and I hate the enemy." But mostly they were people just like us and I felt no hatred, nothing, toward them. They were just doing what they were told to do. And it made me feel sorry for them. They had a belief in their country. They were fighting for their country, just like we were there working for our country too. I worked with the prisoners several times. I was assigned to the recovery room and surgical intensive care, which were combined. The whole hospital was in Quonset huts. I think we had about eight beds in the recovery area, and then we had our nurse's desk, and then on the other end was surgical intensive care. So we would get wounded prisoners in and the sicker ones would stay with us. In addition to GIs we had Vietnamese civilians and Koreans. Once in awhile we'd get South Vietnamese soldiers in our hospital.

We weren't all that interested in talking to the prisoners, but sometimes we found ourselves having these conversations in pidgin English with them. You know, they knew "number one" and "number ten," things like that. It was usually a "Ho Chi Minh number ten, Johnson number one," "No, Johnson number ten, Ho Chi Minh number one." Just things like that. Now as far as real conversations, it was difficult. But I was there at Tet '68 and I was on the night shift. And one night, without any warning, we heard this tremendous explosion. I didn't know what was going on. It sounded like something had landed right outside. I had a prisoner patient who had a trach and I was suctioning him, and of course we had the portable suctions that plugged into the wall. Well, the wall socket was blown out of the wall. And it was just frightening. I didn't know what was going on. It sounded like we were under attack. The thing I remembered we had to do was get the patients under the beds. We had little mattresses we threw down under the beds on the concrete and then we put the patients under the beds. I picked up a seven-months pregnant Vietnamese woman, who had a wound in her side. I picked her up in my arms, went down on one knee, and stuck her under the bed just like that. I was scared. It turned out to have been a large-size ammo dump blowing up about five miles away, no immediate danger to us.

The few times I got to go out into the community, I realized the Vietnamese people were loyal to whoever fed them. It didn't matter who, they just wanted to eat. They could care less about philosophies or type of government. It was obvious that they weren't ready for a democracy. They didn't know what a democracy was. Or is. Before I went over, I had this idea that we needed to get in there and get the war over with. We could win it. We were capable of winning, but you saw quite clearly that we would never be allowed to finish the job, we weren't capable of winning it, and if we won it what would we do with them? It all seemed so useless. I knew that I couldn't do anything about it, that it was going on, and it was . . . and all I could do was help. And it was very gratifying to help. It was a fantastic experience as far as the work was concerned.

Well, I didn't work the emergency room or triage any. And I don't think I could have taken it if I had. I just don't think I could have lasted as long. Maybe I would have lived up to it. But maybe because of the experience I had or because I hadn't had any trauma experience, they did assign me to the ICU and recovery. In the recovery we'd get guys . . . they'd wake up without arms, without legs, but we would go right to work on them. It's time to exercise. PT started immediately. I remember one young lieutenant, though. I forget how many limbs he had lost. It seems like he lost three limbs. It was just so tragic. I tried to write letters for him and do things like that. And my head nurse thought that I . . . that I got a little close, that I shouldn't do as much for him as I did. This was the same kind of thing told to me time and again before I ever joined the Army— that I spent too much time talking with the patients. I think I'm a very caring person. I try to help.

Most of the wounded amputation cases we got in, they probably knew before they ever went into the OR that they weren't going to have that limb when they came out. They probably were told. So many of them were so young. They'd open their eyes and they'd see a round eye. And that's what they called you, a round eye. And it was just . . . it probably made them feel a little better. It was just exciting for them. And it was exciting for me too. In Vietnam the GIs were so grateful that you were there. It was like you were treated special. Very special. Everywhere you went, men were ready to do anything for you. All the time. And that was the one thing I . . . it was a comedown when I came home, to realize that I wasn't special anymore. It was true. Everybody treated you great and you felt like it made you feel . . . feel good. You always felt like you were serving a good purpose.

I remember one day, it had been real quiet. I hadn't been there long. I had a ward master who had been there awhile; he knew the ropes. It was very quiet and we were just walking around looking at all the patients. And we stopped and stood over this Vietnamese; I don't remember whether he was a prisoner or a civilian or what, but he had a piece of skin shot away from his thigh about the size of a saucer. His femoral artery was exposed. It had been grafted back together, but it was there exposed. There was nothing to cover it. And as we stood there and looked, the thing broke. Blood shot up around me . . . I panicked. I ran to get the doctor, while this cool ward master reached over and picked up a piece of gauze and stuck his finger into it. Yes, I ran to get the doctor, and the ward master was in there taking charge. That was the thing about those kinds of hospitals—you didn't always have to run and get the doctor. Those of us who weren't doctors had to do a lot on our own—things we never would have done in civilian hospitals. Well, we got blood started on the guy and they got him to surgery and got it repaired again. But the thing was they repaired it and later on, I wasn't there, but it happened again. This time the patient knew what to do. He reached over and got a piece of gauze and stuck his finger in it.

The only time it really got to me was right toward the end. It was really busy. It was December or November time frame in '68. And we got a lot of fresh wounded. We were short handed. Normally we would only work 12-hour shifts, we got two days a week off. But at this time we were getting no days off, and it was getting to us. And we got all these fresh casualties. This one young guy woke up and he was . . . he lost one or two of his legs, I can't remember. And as soon as he started coming around he started thinking about the battle. He had had a point man that he had just trained and was really super, and he had sent him out. The guy stepped on a mine. It killed him. The rest of them got into a firefight and others had been killed, and he was just furious . . . he was just furious about the whole thing. And he was out of control, and that was just almost more than I could . . . in fact I left. I just told him I couldn't stay there any longer. He was just . . . he was cursing about his buddies being killed. He was crying, and after awhile I was crying too. I wasn't effective anymore. See, I was getting short and wondering how much of my feelings were tied up in this. Not at the time, but later, I wondered why I couldn't tolerate it.

It's hard to explain how everybody felt about everybody. We would sit around and we would just sort of be amazed at how close we all were and we knew it would never happen again. Most of us would never have this experience again.

I made a couple of R&R trips to Hong Kong and Australia during my tour. And Bernard made a trip to the Philippines, right toward the end of my time in Vietnam. As it turned out, his wife flew out there to meet him and they had a big confrontation. When he got back, it was obvious he was distraught. It took him awhile to talk about it, but when he finally did he told me his wife had come prepared to give herself a drug overdose if he did not take her back. And not only that, but she was pregnant by somebody else. And it was just a real, real hard time for him. My feelings were all tied up in him, but I felt as though he had made a commitment because of her situation. Who was I to change it? I didn't feel it was my right to insist on anything else. I felt as though when I left Vietnam that would be the end of it.

I don't know how or with whom she got pregnant, but I guess she discovered life wasn't rosier out there and she wanted her husband back. This was a time when Bernard and I were very close, and this thing just drew us closer, believe it or not. But I felt like it was a dead end, like it would all be over soon. That's the way I left Vietnam. He saw himself as being caught in a trap with nothing he could do about it.

There was nothing for me to do but back off. I just thought "Well, he feels committed, he feels trapped." And I don't think we discussed it. I'm sure we didn't because afterward he said to me several times, "Why didn't you say something?" He wanted to know why I didn't do something to keep him. And I said, "That's your responsibility." It's like he wanted me to insist that he should stay with me. It was almost like he needed the guidance or the suggestion, which I didn't do.

He told her the one stipulation he had for going back was that she had to give this child up for adoption. And she evidently agreed to this in order to get him back. So when he went back to the states they did not live together until after the baby was born. I remember one of my final conversations with him was telling him he'd have children of his own soon. And, of course, he did.

It goes without saying that I was extremely upset. But I had this suspicion all the while that because we were from such different backgrounds it was doubtful that things could work out between us. I felt like I was so different and I think that had a lot to do with my attitude of letting him go and letting him live his own life and not bothering him.

It was very difficult. It was very strange, just like it was all over

and there was nothing to be done about it. The day I left, I went over to the airport and got on a plane with several wounded patients and flew to Cam Ranh Bay. The pilots invited me to sit up in the co-pilot's seat. So I was just sort of in a real haze. When we arrived at Cam Ranh Bay, we boarded a bus. There was this soldier sitting in front of me, and he looked like he was on drugs. He kept talking about what he was going to do when he got back to the states, and he was using some very foul language. I had been pretty naive before going over there, and I guess that part of my personality hadn't changed very much while I was in Vietnam. I had never been ex-posed to worldly things in that way, and hearing him, plus every-thing else that had just gone on with Bernard . . . it just tore me up. I started crying. I cried, cried, and cried. I couldn't get off that bus soon enough. I've thought about this over and over again. Why did I react like that to this guy who's going home to his girlfriend or wife or whatever, and he just wouldn't shut up about it? He just kept talking and talking. I stumbled off the bus and eventually onto the plane. It was just a real haze.

As it turned out, we started writing letters to each other imme-diately. He wrote a lot of letters from there in the time he had left. It was six months before he came home, and he looked me up . . . practically the first thing after he got off the plane. He had gone up country after I left, gotten into some hotter territory. They kept him pretty busy, and he did a lot of helicopter flying. But he went to the Army hospital in Denver, and the next year he got out of the Army altogether. We stopped communicating at this point. I went into re-cruiting and they sent me to Phoenix.

As a recruiter I had to do a lot of traveling, so I was on the road constantly. A few years passed, but one day I found myself in the city where Bernard was living with his wife and practicing medi-cine. This was 1972 or 1973. I called him at his office. I didn't see him. I just called him and we talked. I told him where I was. Not too long after that, he called me. So we had this telephone relationship going, and it's continued ever since. In person, I've seen him only four or five times since then. He's got one daughter; I'm sure he's a fantastic father. I don't think his wife knows of my existence.

I stayed in the Army, I guess because it was a lot of security for me. And I was having fun. My next assignment was in an Army hospital as head nurse in the thoracic-cardiovascular unit, something that was totally new to me. I also had been working in the recovery room for cardiac surgery. It was exciting still. I had lacked a lot of confidence in myself . . . whether I could do difficult things. The military was just shoveling all this stuff on me and I was actually doing it all. My mother always said I was a late bloomer. But things changed in the Army as Vietnam wound down. In wartime the Army has a mission and everything is directed toward accomplishing that. But when the war ends the Army gears into a totally different mode. It's a world of contingencies, "what-ifs." The reality is gone and everything's a question of "how we'd react" and "are we prepared?" I'm better at dealing with concrete things. I thought about getting out but I kept on getting these opportunities that I couldn't turn down. I got an undergraduate degree, and then I came to San Antonio to the Academy of Health Sciences for the advanced course.

Bernard's attitude toward me was one of being concerned about my career, whether I could manage outside the Army. He was concerned to the point of feeling responsible for me. Eventually, when I left the Army, he was worried that I had gotten so used to the security there that I wouldn't be able to make it. That feeling has gone away over the years, because he's seen how well I can do on my own. Picking up the phone and talking with him is like "You don't sound too good today, what's been going on?" or "You sound so much better, I'm glad you're in better shape." It doesn't take much for him to detect what I'm thinking or feeling, or vice-versa.

I met somebody else in the early '70s while I was still in the Army. Again it was the thing of a totally different kind of person, and we were friends for a long time. And this was another guy who was in an unhappy marriage and didn't mean for anything to get started. I don't know if it's my age group or what, but my luck in finding available men has been about zilch. Anyway, Mike was a guy who cared a great deal about me and planned to get a divorce. He got discharged from the military on a medical disability. He had a heart condition and he was dying slowly. He was probably well aware of it. And he intended to leave his wife, but because of his medical disability it was just an impossibility to go through with it. Also he had four children at home. Again, kids come up all the time. And there again, because of my experience as a child with my father leaving, and because of everything . . . it would take a long time to explain these relationships because there were just too, too many things.

Mike was very good for me. He came along at a time when there was nobody around. Nobody at all. And he encouraged my independence and was always there to give me security. He was a nurse, and I met him while I was in recruiting. He had been a prisoner of war in Korea. His heart condition was familial, but I'm sure the months as a prisoner didn't help him much. Mike was a man who could travel around, even though he had a heart condition. He knew he had a limited time to live, but he managed to live life to the fullest. The doctors had been very blunt with him. Maybe today there would be something they could've done for him. But then there was nothing. And Bernard knew about this guy. We talked about the situation all the time, not at inappropriate times, but we talked. He knew this was going on and who this guy was. Bernard was my confidante. Bernard realized the guy couldn't last long. Things came to a head in 1979 and 1980. I got out of the Army and Mike died shortly thereafter.

I was devastated. And the first person I called was Bernard. I had to share it with someone, and there was only Bernard. It devastated him too. He came to visit me in San Antonio six months after Mike died. I was very, very nervous and he was trying to be Mr. Cool. I picked him up at his hotel downtown and brought him back to my house. And it was like it was just a big front till we got back home and then that's when I certainly collapsed. My emotions had been on the brink for a long time, and it all just poured right out of me. He was Mr. Wiseman, oh, yes. He comforted me and said, "Let's talk."

I don't remember what he said to me. I don't remember the particulars. It was basically "It's not as if life won't go on," or "Life simply has to go on." It wasn't what he said that mattered as much as the fact that he was there. It put him in a real dilemma. In fact, he had a real emotional crisis after that himself, and I don't know if his own situation got mixed up in it or not. He went through an emotional crisis, close to a nervous breakdown, and had to be hospitalized. I guess I had put pressure on him, you know, "Will this (relationship) ever be?" I think that's what really drove him down. It was trying to sort out just how he felt, what he wanted to do. I'm surmising a lot of things because there's a lot he hasn't told me. There's a lot I don't feel like I want to hear. Sometimes it's better not to know what's happening on the other end. I've told him that.

Vietnam is what brought us together in the first place and I guess ultimately it's what drew us back to each other. It always goes back to that. It seems like we just pick up where we left off. It's just like there's never any gap; or when we see each other it's just like it was the last time, as if we saw each other yesterday. We were so close in Vietnam and we shared so much. I don't communicate with anybody else from that time. I occasionally meet people who were there around the same time, but it's not the same as someone you actually knew over there.

Our getting back together again wasn't intentional. It was just like "I want to see you again." We discussed it at great length—the emotional impact on each other, whether it would be worth it or not. At this point, it's not like I'm waiting for him or we're planning for the next time we see each other. It's nothing like that. He alludes to these possible rendezvous, you know, "I'm going to be at such and such a place next week," and I say, "That's nice." Sometimes I tell him I'm not capable of handling this emotionally. There's a great deal of ambiguity between us, to say the least. I don't want the pain of coming back down from the high of being with him. I'd just rather stay this way until such a time that it could be permanent. There will always be a special feeling, no matter whether it never works out or whether it does. I guess in the back of my mind I see the day when his children are grown and he's free.

If he ever finds himself free and if he wants me, then I think that's all it would take for it to work. But he has to want this relationship to go forward. That would mean a big break for him, and I don't know whether he could do it. I don't know whether I could either. I think a lot about the differences between us. They are as real now as they were 18 years ago when we first met.

I have a friend who calls me "the rescuer." You know, her view of me is that I rescued the men in my life in much the same way I rescued the wounded back in Vietnam . . . as though I had some lifelong commitment to salvaging hardship cases in impossible situations. I've tried to analyze myself and I constantly wonder why

I'm like I am. Despite my lack of confidence, I think I am a very strong person. I think my mother is a very strong person, and I think I probably get that from her. And I notice that with my female friends, I seem to be there for them. They get under stress or something like that, and I might say, "Let's stand back and look at this objectively." I think I'm very stable, yes.

It bothers me that I've been more or less a failure in certain parts of my life. I haven't done the expected. I'd hate to think of myself as seeking out people who give me no options. I just think that's a weakness, and I don't like to think of myself that way. That it has turned out that way to some extent, I can't fully explain.

I know I'm a strong person and I know I withstood some very devastating things during my life, starting with my father leaving us. You can't let things get you down. Despite the way it might seem, I guess I've never been a dependent person. It seems like a lot of women find men who want to save them. I'm sort of the opposite. I think the men that I have been close to have been strong men. It's just that . . . they've needed me. I don't go around looking for people to rescue. But I guess I stand out like a beacon to people who need someone to console them. Some of them wound up getting very, very close. But I'm selective. I couldn't deal with everyone's problems. I just don't have enough of that particular quality to go around. The thing is I know who I've been able to take care of—the wounded: physically, emotionally, and otherwise. But who takes care of me? Who do I lean on? Well, my church, I guess. When everything else has failed, it's been my faith in God that's seen me through. And I think that's probably sufficient.